The Great House of Birds

The Great House of Birds

CLASSIC WRITINGS
ABOUT BIRDS

Edited by John Hay

SIERRA CLUB BOOKS • SAN FRANCISCO

I am especially grateful to two people who helped me in the indispensable task of typing and editing the material in this anthology, namely, Mary Fisher Fisk of New Pensmith in Dennis, Mass., and Emily Wheeler, the exceptionally clear-eyed and perceptive copy editor for Sierra Club Books, from Amherst, N.Y.

LIBRARY OF CONGRESS CATALOGING IN PUBLICATION DATA
The great house of birds: classic writings about birds / edited by John Hay.
p.   cm.
ISBN 0-87156-855-1 (cloth : alk. paper)
1. Birds.   2. Birds in literature.   I. Hay, John, 1915–
QL699.G74   1996
598–dc20   92-5925

Production by Janet Vail · Jacket and book design by Amy Evans · Composition by Wilsted & Taylor

Printed in the United States on acid-free paper containing a minimum of 50% recovered waste paper of which at least 10% of the fiber content is post-consumer waste.

10   9   8   7   6   5   4   3   2   1

Contents

2. The Language of Birds

3. Art and Ritual

To my dear wife, Kristi,
number one feeder of the birds,
and of the rest of us

Foreword

The selections in this anthology are not intended to represent the best of nature writing, past or present, but to illuminate a subject which long preceded the written word. What I try to do is balance myth, poetry, and natural history so as to reflect human contact with birds on many different levels. This needs far more room than I have available, and readers will inevitably think of a great deal of valuable material that I have left out. I only hope that this method will have the advantage of all it suggests. Certainly, life lists of birds and the latest information about them are never quite enough to satisfy our natural curiosity and our need to know more.

Why do birds get as much attention as they do? Symbolically at least, their presence is accepted by most people, and the ranks of the bird watchers are increasing every year. At the same time, those with "bird brains" are dismissed as insignificant. Birds' lives seem foreign to us. The idea that birds are indispensable to the earth's vitality—and therefore to our own—is not generally accepted. They must survive our world as best they can. After all, those who advocate the protection of wildlife and the conservation of habitats are often faced with the question, Which do you want, birds or people? Little evidence proves that children or adults automatically favor the feathered race; very often they dislike it. So where does the affinity come from?

Niko Tinbergen, the famous ethnologist and author of *The Herring Gull's World,* contends that "we can understand the behavior of other birds better than that of most other animals," since our sensory equipment, especially our eyes and ears, is similar to theirs. Understanding, of course, does not always include sympathy. I suspect that we are deeply attracted to birds through the spirit, a realm which does not easily admit exact definitions, but whose depths are consistent. Birds migrate far beyond our land-based abilities and have always been associated with the aspiration of flight, in reality or in dreams. They also engage in courtship rituals, during which they often dance and present offerings to each other, displaying behavior not dissimilar to our own. Their spontaneity is enchanting; their songs are as welcome as the springtime.

Birds fly away from us, with an unspoken invitation to follow after. At the same time, each of their wonderfully varied species has the deepest kind of alliance with the earth. Nearly everywhere, they are declarative, quick, drab or extravagantly colorful, suited to every kind of environment. As fish are facets of water, birds reflect the global surfaces.

So it is their constant presence, and at the same time their elusiveness, which intrigues us. The question of whether birds think, or love, or react intelligently, according to our standards, is restricted by our own self-conscious experience. We see them through the lens of our human limitations, and so they elude us. What we still do not know about how birds migrate, or about how they react to the atmosphere and each other, is as wide open as everything we do not know about ourselves.

One might say that in their continued existence and *otherness* lie our opportunity to keep our vital earth relationships alive. The question is not how important birds are assessed to be in terms of our own lives and culture, it is whether or not we exist in a healthy state without them.

In a sense, all those who have contributed to this book, from ancient seafarer to present-day writer, come together as searchers and interpreters, each in their own style and calling. They are engaged in an inner dialogue with a race which occupied and explored the planet long before us. Understanding birds, as well as we are able to, involves a present as well as a historical attempt to understand ourselves. An individuals, we are easily lost in our world. What helps to save us is equation with other forms of life which are one in the unanimity of being, though differing mysteriously from our own. The birds come in out of a great past to give continuity to the present.

Part One

Flight

Wings we have with us all the time, regardless of our feelings about birds. There are wings on postage stamps, on many statues and public buildings, and on our omnipresent and constantly "improved" automobiles. Wings fly with us in airplanes and are worn by Air Force pilots. In the course of redesigning modern airplanes, the flight of gulls was studied intensively.

Whatever impressed civilization to go so far and so fast but the powers of flight as seen in birds, creatures of sudden appearances and disappearances, often flying so high that they are lost to sight behind a cloud. An ancient fascination with flight seizes us, and we wear it on our persons. People once thought that the birds must commune with higher powers. In modern times, when people tend to feel superior to other animals, birds are seldom given much credit. We are the ones who landed on the moon, who explore outer space.

Still, our assumptions as bipeds, the "two leggeds," as the Native Americans called us, upright on the ground, often exceed our pretensions. Like Icarus, we may fly too close to

the sun, burn our wings, and plunge to our death in the sea.
So myth and mechanics are joined in one. The power to fly
alone eludes us. Bird watchers today, when they pull out an
advanced pair of binoculars to get a closer look at their
quarries, are merely pursuing the secrets of birds with up-
to-date tools.

Wherever they can be found, the "winged ones" are
quick and close inspectors of their surroundings as well as
masters of the earth's atmosphere and its great distances.
Earth born, sky borne, the birds carry space and time upon
their wings. They have an enviable inner sense of weather
changes, and their lives and ceremonies are disciplined by
the seasons. There could be no better guides to "a sense of
place."

The Terns

MARY OLIVER

The birds shrug off
the slant air,
they plunge into the sea
and vanish
under the glassy edges
of the water,
and then come back,
flying out of the waves,
as white as snow,
shaking themselves,
shaking the little silver fish,
crying out
in their own language,
voices like rough bells—
it's wonderful
and it happens whenever
the tide starts its gushing

journey back, every morning
or afternoon.
This is a poem
about death,
about the heart blanching
in its fold of shadows
because it knows
someday it will be
the fish and the wave
and no longer itself—
it will be those white wings,
flying in and out
of the darkness
but not knowing it—
this is a poem about loving
the world and everything in it:
the self, the perpetual muscle,
the passage in and out, the bristling
swing of the sea.

FROM *The House of Light*

Skyey Thoughts

☙

This extract from The Land of Journey's Ending *illustrates Mary Austin's ability, in a sensitive, lyrical style, to express her feelings for a region where the human spirit has been an inescapable part of the land itself for thousands of years. Her book followed her earlier classic,* Land of Little Rain.

☙

The notice of birds by the aboriginal mind travels a curiously intricate path, taking value from association with the mysterious formless powers, as the eagle with the Thunder, twin dwellers of the upper air.

Thus eagles' plumes and bluebirds' feathers become emblems of skyey approval. Eagle down is the sign of man's secret godward aspiration, and the milky way a drift of snowy feathers where the lesser gods make prayer plumes for the elder. By association with the water-holes where they resort

to feed fat on the small rodents coming to drink, snakes become water symbols, and the plumed serpent, wriggling like
the lightning against the curtain of the dark cloud, the pa-
tron of the Water-Sources. There are, however, not nearly so
many thick rattlers at the water-holes to-day as when our
Ancients named them guardians of the springs. Often the
snake-dancers of Hopi have to make up the kiva's quota
with harmless gopher-snakes, and striped frequenters of the
melon fields.

I am Indian enough, I hope, not to miss the birds that
are place marks; shrill, chittering Texas nighthawks above
the water holes, jewel-green hummingbirds that haunt the
hundred-belled yucca bocata. Also Indian enough to leave
nameless and unnoticed a hundred singers, to observe the
elf owl in the sahuaro, drawing its spread wing like a lady's
fan, for protective cover before topaz glittering eyes. . . .
Witch, O witch . . . !

> With this raven's plume,
> With this owl's feather
> I will make Black Prayers for her
> Who takes my man from me. . . .
> With this owl's plume
> With this raven's feather!

Now and then you find a horned lark, which, like the
lark that Shelley heard, rises as it sings, treasured in a cage
at the pueblo, for which the children gather grasshoppers,
threading them on grass stems. But for the most part it is
the literary interest which is served by birds, man making
them to stand for his thought in upper airy reaches of his
mind, long before he had any other use for those he could
not use for food. So because the track of the road-runner's
feet turns two ways, he ties the shining feathers on the cra-
dle board to confuse the evil spirits coming to trouble the

child's mind, as the four-toed sign of the cross protects from harm.

Anybody who cared for birds for their own sake, however, would find all that his liking needs in the crested ranges of the Mogollon Rim, which is the farthest north for tropic birds, and farthest south for birds of the arctic in their yearly migrations. In the Chiricahuas there is a thick-billed parrot with splashes of poppy red upon his wings, and little green macaws, whose feathers make the knot like a sprouting corn hill, tied in the dark locks of the corn-dancers, talking to themselves among the yellow pines. Or in the Alpine island tops of sacred mountains with the whistling marmot and the rabbit-eared coney, one discovers the snowy ptarmigan turning rock-moss color to protect its rock-speckled eggs, lacking all other cover between them and the sky. Between seasons, great fleets of water-fowl sail the wind rivers above the Colorado draw, or gather along the estuary, waiting for the ebb to uncover springs of sweet water among the reedy dunes, and pelicans perform their stately dance along the medanos, clotted with satin shiny clumps of *rosas San Juan.* Once the sandhill crane could be heard whooping by unfrequented watercourses, but I doubt you will hear that bugling call anywhere now except among the ghost-invoking cries of the Navajo fire-dancers, crying "Come, Come, Come!" Thus I might name a hundred species from the broad-tailed humming-birds, droning like bees about the holy peaks of San Francisco Mountains, to the hermit thrush singing at evening on steep, dark-forested slopes the sacrament of desire, only to find that for you, as for our Ancients, and Keats and Shelley, birds serve best when they serve as symbols for free roving, skyey thought.

FROM *The Land of Journey's Ending*

The Windhover

GERARD MANLEY HOPKINS

To Christ our Lord

I caught this morning morning's minion, king-
   dom of daylight's dauphin, dapple-dawn-drawn Falcon,
      in his riding
   Of the rolling level underneath him steady air, and
      striding
High there, how he rung upon the rein of a wimpling wing
In his ecstasy! then off, off forth on swing,
   As a skate's heel sweeps smooth on a bow-bend: the hurl
      and gliding
   Rebuffed the big wind. My heart in hiding
Stirred for a bird,—the achieve of, the mastery of the thing!

Brute beauty and valour and act, oh, air, pride, plume, here
  Buckle! AND the fire that breaks from thee then, a billion
Times told lovelier, more dangerous, O my chevalier!

  No wonder of it: shéer plód makes plough down sillion
Shine, and blue-bleak embers, ah my dear,
  Fall, gall themselves, and gash gold-vermilion.

FROM *A Gerard Manley Hopkins Reader*

The Peregrine

J. A. BAKER

The Peregrine Falcon—"duck hawk" in America—almost ex-tirpated because of pesticides and still endangered, was origi-nally named for its erratic migratory movements, which were reminiscent of the "peregrine Christians" who journeyed to the Holy Sepulcher. It is the faucon pelerin *in French, and the* Wanderfalke *in German. The Latin derivation is* peregrinus, *a traveler in foreign parts. Its range is worldwide. A society that destroys such a bird, in its beauty and audacity, is abandoning a fellow pilgrim on earth's journey. The following is a detailed account of a daily, passionate engagement between a man and a bird.*

☙

OCTOBER 12TH: Dry leaves wither and shine, green of the oak is fading, elms are barred with luminous gold.

There was fog, but the south wind blew it away. The sun-burnt sky grew hot. Damp air moved over dusty earth. The north was a haze of blue, the south bleached white. Larks sang up into the warmth, or flashed along furrows. Gulls and lapwings drifted from plough to plough.

Autumn peregrines come inland from the estuaries to bathe in the stony shallows of brook or river. Between eleven o'clock and one they rest in dead trees to dry their feathers, preen, and sleep. Perching stiff and erect, they look like gnarled and twisted oak. To find them, one must learn the shapes of all the valley trees, till anything added becomes, at once, a bird. Hawks hide in dead trees. They grow out of them like branches.

At midday I flushed the tiercel from an elm by the river. Against brown fields, brown leaves, brown mist low to the skyline, he was hard to see. He looked much smaller than the two crows that chased him. But when he rose against the white sky he was bigger, and easier to focus. Quickly he circled higher, slewing away from his course at sudden tangents, baffling the clumsy crows. They always overshot him, and laboured heavily to regain the distance lost. They called, rolling out the r's of their guttural high-pitched 'prruk, prruk,' their hawk-mobbing cry. When mobbed, the peregrine beats its wings deeply and rhythmically. They bounce from the air, with silent slaps, like a lapwing's. This deliberate pulse of evasion is beautiful to watch; one breathes in time to it; the effect is hypnotic.

The tiercel turned and twisted in the sun. The undersides of his wings flashed in sword-glints of silver. His dark eyes shone, and the bare skin around them glittered like salt. At five hundred feet the crows gave up, planing back to the trees on outspread wings. The hawk rose higher, and flew fast to the north, gliding smoothly up and round into long soaring circles, till he was hidden in blue haze. Plover volleyed from the fields and fretted the horizon with the dark susurrus of their wings.

Throughout the glaring afternoon, I sat at the southern end of the big field by the river. The sun was hot on my back, and the dry sand-and-clay coloured field shimmered in desert haze. Partridge coveys stood out upon the shining surface like rings of small black stones. When the peregrine circled above them, the partridge rings shrank inward. Lapwings rose and fled. They had been hidden in the furrows, as the hawk was hidden in the shiny corrugations of the sky.

Crows flew up again to chase the hawk away, and the three birds drifted east. Dry feathered and more buoyant now, the tiercel did not beat his wings, but simply soared in the abundant warmth of air. He dodged easily the sudden rushes of the crows, and swooped at them with waggling snipey wings. One crow planed back to earth, but the other plodded on, beating heavily round, a hundred feet below the hawk. When both were very small and high above the wooded hill, the hawk slowed down to let the crow catch up. They dashed at each other, tangling and flinging away, swooping up to regain the height they lost. Rising and fighting, they circled out of sight. Long afterwards the crow came floating back, but the hawk had gone. Half-way to the estuary I found him again, circling among thousands of starlings. They ebbed and flowed about him, bending and flexing sinuously across the sky, like the black funnel of a whirlwind. They carried the tormented hawk towards the coast, till all were suddenly scorched from sight in the horizon's gold corona.

The tide was rising in the estuary; sleeping waders crowded the saltings; plover were restless. I expected the hawk to drop from the sky, but he came low from inland. He was a skimming black crescent, cutting across the saltings, sending up a cloud of dunlin dense as a swarm of bees. He drove up between them, black shark in shoals of silver fish, threshing and plunging. With a sudden stab down he was clear of the swirl and was chasing a solitary dunlin up into the sky. The dunlin seemed to come slowly back to the hawk. It passed into his dark outline, and did not re-appear. There was no brutality, no violence. The hawk's foot reached out, and gripped, and squeezed, and quenched the dunlin's heart as effortlessly as a man's finger extinguishing an insect. Languidly, easily, the hawk glided down to an elm on the island to plume and eat his prey.

OCTOBER 14TH: One of those rare autumn days, calm under high cloud, mild, with patches of distant sunlight circling round and rafters of blue sky crumbling into mist. Elms and oaks still green, but some now scorched with gold. A few leaves falling. Choking smoke from stubble burning.

High tide was at three o'clock, lifting along the southern shore of the estuary. Snipe shuddering from the dykes. White glinting water welling in, mouthing the stones of the sea-wall. Moored boats pecking at the water. Dark red glasswort shining like drowned blood.

Curlew coming over from the island in long flat shields of birds, changing shape like waves upon the shore, long V's widening and narrowing their arms. Redshanks shrill and vehement; never still, never silent. The faint, insistent sadness of grey plover calling. Turnstone and dunlin rising. Twenty greenshank calling, flying high; grey and white as gulls, as sky. Bar-tailed godwits flying with curlew, with knot, with plover; seldom alone, seldom settling; snuffling eccentrics; long-nosed, loud-calling sea-rejoicers; their call a snorting, sneezing, mewing, spitting bark. Their thin up-curved bills turn, their heads turn, their shoulders and whole bodies turn, their wings waggle. They flourish their rococo flight above the surging water.

Screaming gulls corkscrewing high under cloud. Islands blazing with birds. A peregrine rising and falling. God-wits ricocheting across water, tumbling, towering. A pere-grine following, swooping, clutching. Godwit and pere-grine darting, dodging; stitching land and water with flickering shuttle. Godwit climbing, dwindling, tiny, gone: peregrine diving, perching, panting, beaten.

Tide going out, wigeon cropping zostera, herons lanky in shallows. Sheep on the sea-wall grazing. Revolve the long estuary through turning eyes. Let the water smooth out its healing line, like touch of dock on nettled finger. Leave the wader-teeming skies, soft over still water, arched light.

OCTOBER 15TH: Fog cleared quickly after one o'clock, and sun shone. The peregrine arrived from the east an hour later. It was seen by sparrows, lapwings, starlings, and woodpigeons, but not by me. I watched and waited in a field near the ford, trying to be as still and patient as the heron that was standing in stubble and waiting for mice to run within reach of his down-chopping bill. Bullfinches called by the brook; swallows flickered round my head. A covey of magpies muttered in hawthorns and then dispersed, dragging up their baggy broomstick tails, catapulting them-selves forward from each flurry of wingbeats, sagging on to air at the angle of a well-thrown discus. Thousands of star-lings came into the valley to gather by the river before flying to roost.

At half-past four, blackbirds began to scold in the hedges,

and red-legged partridges called. I scanned the sky, and found two peregrines—tiercel and falcon—flying high above the ford, chased by crows. The crows soon gave up, but the peregrines flew round for another twenty minutes, in wide random circles. They made many abrupt-angled turns, so that they were never more than a quarter of a mile from the ford. They flew with deep, measured wingbeats— the tiercel's quicker than the falcon's—but they did not move fast. The tiercel flew higher, and constantly swooped down at the falcon, shuddering his wings violently. She avoided these rushes by veering slightly aside. Sometimes both birds slowed till they were almost hovering; then they gradually increased their speed again.

The detail of their plumage was difficult to see, but their moustachial bars seemed as prominent at a distance as they did when close. The falcon's breast was golden tinted, barred laterally with blackish brown. Her upper parts were a blend of blue-black and brown, so she was probably a second winter bird moulting into adult plumage.

This was the peregrines' true hunting time; an hour and a half to sunset, with the western light declining and the early dusk just rising above the eastern skyline. I thought at first that the peregrines were ringing up to gain height, but they went on circling for so long that obviously some sort of sexual pursuit and display was involved. The birds around me believed they were in danger. Blackbirds and partridges were never silent; woodpigeons, lapwings, and jackdaws scattered from the fields and left the area completely; mallard flew up from the brook.

After twenty minutes the hawks began to fly faster. They rose higher, and the tiercel stopped swooping at the falcon. They circled once, at great speed, and then flew east without turning back. They flickered out of sight towards the

estuary, vanishing into the grey dusk a thousand feet above
the hill. They were hunting.

OCTOBER 16TH: Waders slept in the spray that leapt from
the waves along the shingle ridges. They lined the hot furrows of the inland fields, where dust was blowing. Dunlin,
ringed plover, knot and turnstone, faced the wind and sun,
clustered together like white pebbles on brown earth.

A roaring southerly gale drove waves to lash the high sea-
wall, flinging their spray up through the air above. On the
lee side of the wall the long, dry grass was burning. Gasps
of yellow flame and northward streaming smoke jetted
away in the wind. There was a fierce anguish of heat, like
a beast in pain. The short grass on top of the wall glowed
orange and black; it hissed when the salt spray thudded
down. Under a torrid sky, and in the strength of the sun,
water and fire were rejoicing together.

When the waders suddenly flew, I looked beyond them
and saw a peregrine lashing down from the northern sky.
By the high hunched shoulders, and the big head bent between, and the long, flickering shudder-up and shake-out
of the wings, I knew that this was the tiercel. He flew
straight towards me, and his eyes seemed to stare into mine.
Then they widened in recognition of my hostile human
shape. The long wings wrenched and splayed as the hawk
swerved violently aside.

I saw his colours clearly in the brilliant light: back and
secondaries rich burnt sienna; primaries black; underparts ochreous yellow, streaked with arrowheads of tawny
brown. Down the pale cheeks the long dark triangles of
the moustachial lobes depended from the polished sun-
reflecting eyes.

Through the smoke, through the spray, he glided over the

wall in a smooth outpouring, like water gliding over stone. The waders shimmered to earth, and slept. The hawk's plumage stained through shadows of smoke, gleamed like mail in glittering spray. He flew out in the grip of the gale, flicking low across the rising tide. He slashed at a floating gull, and would have plucked it from the water if it had not flown up at once. He flickered out into the light, a small dark blemish diminishing along the great sword of sun-dazzle that lay across the estuary from the south.

By dusk the wind had passed to the north. The sky was clouded, the water low and calm, the fires dying. Out of the misty darkening north, a hundred mallard climbed into the brighter sky, towering above the sunset, far beyond the peregrine that watched them from the shore and the gunners waiting low in the marsh.

OCTOBER 18TH: The valley a damp cocoon of mist; rain drifting through; jackdaws elaborating their oddities of voice and fight, their rackety pursuits, their febrile random feeding; golden plover calling in the rain.

When a crescendo of crackling jackdaws swept into the elms and was silent, I knew that the peregrine was flying. I followed it down to the river. Thousands of starlings sat on pylons and cables, bills opening wide as each bird had his bubbly, squeaky say. Crows watched for the hawk, and blackbirds scolded. After five minutes' alertness the crows relaxed, and released their frustration by swooping at starlings. Blackbirds stopped scolding.

The fine rain was heavy and cold, and I stood by a hawthorn for shelter. At one o'clock, six fieldfares flew into the bush, ate some berries, and flew on again. Their feathers were dark and shining with damp. It was quiet by the river. There was only the faint whisper of the distant weir and

the soft gentle breathing of the wind and rain. A monoto-
nous 'keerk, keerk, keerk' sound began, somewhere to the
west. It went on for a long time before I recognised it. At
first I thought it was the squeak and puff of a mechanical
water-pump, but when the sound came nearer I realised
that it was a peregrine screeching. This saw-like rasping
continued for twenty minutes, gradually becoming feebler
and spasmodic. Then it stopped. The peregrine chased a
crow through the misty fields and into the branches of a
dead oak. As they swooped up to perch, twenty woodpigeons hurtled out of the tree as though they had been fired
from it. The crow hopped and sidled along a branch till it
was within pecking distance of the peregrine, who turned
to face it, lowering his head and wings into a threatening
posture. The crow retreated, and the hawk began to call
again. His slow, harsh, beaky, serrated cry came clearly
across to me through a quarter of a mile of saturated misty
air. There is a fine challenging ring to a peregrine's call
when there are cliffs or mountains or wide river valleys to
give it echo and timbre. A second crow flew up, and the
hawk stopped calling. When both crows rushed at him, he
flew at once to an overhead wire, where they left him alone.

He looked down at the stubble field in front of him,
sleepy but watchful. Gradually he became more alert and
intent, restlessly clenching and shifting his feet on the wire.
His feathers were ruffled and rain-sodden, draggling down
his chest like plaited tawny and brown ropes. He drifted
lightly to the field, rose with a mouse, and flew to a distant
tree to eat it. He came back to the same place an hour later,
and again he sat watching the field; solid, hunched, and
bulky with rain. His large head inclined downward, and his
eyes probed and unravelled and sorted the intricate mazes
of stubbled furrows and rank-spreading weeds. Suddenly

he leapt forward into the spreading net of his wings, and flew quickly down to the field. Something was running towards the safety of the ditch at the side. The hawk dropped lightly upon it. Four wings fluttered together, then two were suddenly still. The hawk flew heavily to the centre of the field, dangling a dead moorhen from his foot. It had wandered too far from cover, as moorhens so often do in their search for food, and it had forgotten the enemy that does not move. The bird out of place is always the first to die. Terror seeks out the odd, and the sick, and the lost.

The hawk turned his back to the rain, half spread his wings, and began to feed. For two or three minutes his head stayed down, moving slightly from side to side, as he plucked feathers from the breast of his prey. Then both head and neck moved steadily, regularly, up and down, as he skewered flesh with his notched and pointed bill and dragged lumps of it away from the bone by jerking his head sharply upward. Each time his head came up he looked quickly to left and right before descending again to his food. After ten minutes, this up and down motion became slower, and the pauses between each gulp grew longer. But desultory feeding went on for fifteen minutes more.

When the hawk was still, and his hunger apparently satisfied, I went carefully across the soaking wet grass towards him. He flew at once, carrying the remains of his prey, and was soon hidden in the blinding rain. He begins to know me, but he will not share his kill.

FROM *The Peregrine*

The Humming Bird in Colonial America

HECTOR ST. JOHN DE CRÈVECOEUR

St. John de Crèvecoeur was born in Caen, Normandy, in 1725. After traveling to America, he apparently left Quebec after the defeat of the French army under Montcalm and then entered the British colonies. He followed the Hudson River south and stayed for some time in Pennsylvania before moving to New York, where he bought a farm. He loved to wander and was at the same time keenly interested in the life around him in the New World.

The famous book, Letters of an American Farmer, *by this early naturalist was first published in England in 1782. An American edition followed, published in 1793. He died in 1813. The town of St. Johnsbury, Vermont, is named in his honor.*

One anecdote I must relate, the circumstances of which are as true as they are singular. One of my constant walks when I am at leisure, is in my lowlands, where I have the pleasure of seeing my cattle, horses, and colts. Exuberant grass replenishes all my fields, the best representative of our wealth; in the middle of that tract I have cut a ditch eight feet wide, the banks of which nature adorns every spring with the wild salendine, and other flowering weeds, which on these luxuriant grounds shoot up to a great height. Over this ditch I have erected a bridge, capable of bearing a loaded waggon; on each side I carefully sow every year some grains of hemp, which rise to the height of fifteen feet, so strong and so full of limbs as to resemble young trees: I once ascended one of them four feet above the ground. These produce natural arbours, rendered often still more compact by the assistance of an annual creeping plant which we call a vine, that never fails to entwine itself among their branches, and always produces a very desirable shade. From this simple grove I have amused myself an hundred times in observing the great number of humming birds with which our country abounds: the wild blossoms everywhere attract the attention of these birds, which like bees subsist by suction. From this retreat I distinctly watch them in all their various attitudes; but their flight is so rapid, that you cannot distinguish the motion of their wings. On this little bird nature has profusely lavished her most splendid colours; the most perfect azure, the most beautiful gold, the most dazzling red, are for ever in contrast, and help to embellish the plumes of his majestic head. The richest palette of the most luxuriant painter could never invent anything to be compared to the variegated tints, with which this insect bird is arrayed. Its bill is as long and as sharp as a coarse sewing needle; like the bee, nature has taught it to find out in the

calix of flowers and blossoms, those mellifluous particles
that serve it for sufficient food; and yet it seems to leave
them untouched, undeprived of anything that our eyes can
possibly distinguish. When it feeds, it appears as if immov-
able though continually on the wing; and sometimes, from
what motives I know not, it will tear and lacerate flowers
into a hundred pieces: for, strange to tell, they are the most
irascible of the feathered tribe. Where do passions find
room in so diminutive a body? They often fight with the
fury of lions, until one of the combatants falls a sacrifice
and dies. When fatigued, it has often perched within a few
feet of me, and on such favourable opportunities I have surveyed it with the most minute attention. Its little eyes appear like diamonds, reflecting light on every side: most
elegantly finished in all parts it is a miniature work of our
great parent; who seems to have formed it the smallest, and
at the same time the most beautiful of the winged species.

FROM *Letters of an American Farmer*

The Flight of the Hummingbird

ALEXANDER F. SKUTCH

The following is taken from the Life of the Hummingbird *by the renowned naturalist of Central America, Alexander Skutch. From his house in Costa Rica he has spent many years in observing the tropical birds of the rainforest. Hummingbirds, which migrate in season from tropical regions of Central and South America to Alaska on the West Coast and Canada on the East, make journeys that seem prodigious for this tiny bird. Hummingbirds live at a high pitch, with heartbeats that can exceed twelve hundred a minute during periods of intense activity, or drop down to about five hundred. Nevertheless, they may survive from 9 to 10 years in sheltered conditions.*

The flight of hummingbirds is no less wonderful than their refulgent plumage. Watch a hummingbird as it sucks nectar from a spike or panicle of long, tubular flowers pointing in all directions. Now it hovers motionless on wings vibrated into unsubstantial blurs, while its long bill probes the depths of a corolla. Its drink finished, it flies backward to withdraw its bill from the tube, hovers briefly, then perhaps shifts sideways in the air, to place itself squarely in front of another blossom. With equal facility it adjusts its level up or down to reach higher or lower flowers. If the flower points sideward, the bird hovers with its body only slightly inclined; if it points downward, the hummingbird with equal ease drinks with its hovering body nearly vertical and its bill directed straight up. When it has satisfied its thirst, it may pivot around on a fixed point in the air before it darts swiftly away.

Although heavier than air, the hummingbird appears to be in perfect equilibrium with it, like a fish in water; with equal ease it moves in any direction, forward or backward, up or down, to the right or to the left, as well as pivoting on a stationary axis. No other bird can do all these things. The only limitation to the hummingbird's competence in the air is its inability to soar on motionless wings; this is a capacity reserved for larger birds with broader wings.

Among the hummingbird's other accomplishments is its ability to achieve practically full speed at the instant it takes wing. Indeed, it has been said to start flying before it leaves its perch; far from using the perch as a resistance against which to push with its feet and spring forward, it may lift a slender twig slightly at the moment of leaving it. Similarly, it has no need to reduce velocity as it approaches a perch; it may reach the perch at full speed and stop abruptly, in a way that would be disastrous to an airplane or a heavier bird.

Some of the hummingbird's flying abilities are useful not only when visiting flowers but also while nesting. Certain hummingbirds, notably the hermits, fasten their nest beneath the arching tip of a palm leaf, which they always face while incubating eggs or brooding nestlings. To leave, they start beating their wings while still sitting, fly upward and backward until clear of nest and leaf, then reverse and dart away. To return to the nest, hummingbirds of all kinds fly right into it instead of alighting on the rim or nearby and hopping in, as other birds do. By the time the newly arrived hummingbird's wings are folded, it is already incubating. When a white-eared hummingbird wishes to change her orientation in the nest, she sets her wings in motion, rises up slightly, and pivots around. When she wishes to turn her eggs, she flies upward and backward about one inch, to alight on the rim facing inward.

Another remarkable feat of the hummingbird is flying upside-down. If suddenly assailed from the front, as while visiting a flower, it may turn a backward somersault by flipping its spread tail forward, dart a short distance with its wings in reverse and feet upward, then roll over and continue in normal flight.

To understand how a hummingbird can do all these things, we must consider the structure of its flying apparatus, especially the wings and the muscles that move them. As already mentioned when comparing hummingbirds and swifts, the wings of both are practically all hand, the part that corresponds to our arms being greatly reduced in size. The hummingbird's hand bears ten large flight feathers, known as primaries, but the forearm bears only six or seven such feathers, called secondaries—whereas a soaring bird, such as the albatross, has ten primaries and about forty secondaries.

The hummingbird's short arm bones form a rigid V; the elbow and wrist joints allow little flexure. The shoulder joint, on the contrary, is extremely supple, permitting not only movement in all directions but also axial rotation of the whole wing through about 180 degrees. (Our own shoulder joint permits us to swing our arms about as freely as a hummingbird moves its wings, but permits only slight axial rotation of the whole arm; although some of us can revolve our hands through nearly 360 degrees, the forearm does most of the rotation.) The concentration of the wings' weight near the base where the larger bones are situated facilitates changes in their position relative to the hummingbird's body.

The hummingbird has a relatively large breastbone with a prominent keel. The muscles attached to it that move the wings are exceedingly well developed, accounting for 25 or 30 per cent of the bird's weight. Moreover, the elevator muscles, which lift the wing, are about half as heavy as the depressor muscles, whose contraction makes the downstroke. In most birds the elevator muscles are only from one-tenth to one-twentieth as heavy as the depressor muscles.

These structural peculiarities give the hummingbird its exceptional control of all its movements in the air. In other birds only the downstroke gives lift or propulsion, the upstroke, made with the wings partly folded and the primaries separated to diminish air resistance, is a movement of recovery made with weak muscles, unavoidable, but contributing little to the bird's progress. In hummingbirds, on the contrary, both strokes are made with rigidly extended wings moved by powerful muscles. By altering the angle at which the wings cleave the air, both strokes are made to provide lift and propulsion.

When the hummingbird hovers motionless, its rapidly beating wings move forward and backward rather than up and down, their tips tracing a flat figure of eight in the air. With each reversal of the beat, the wings are pivoted through about 180 degrees, so that the front edge always leads and on the backstroke the undersides of the flight feathers are uppermost. Accordingly, while both forward and back strokes give lift, they cancel whatever tendency to horizontal displacement each may have and hold the bird in a single spot with no evident oscillation.

The great majority of hummingbirds appear unable to walk or hop. They scarcely ever alight on the ground, and to move a few inches on a branch, they fly. They depend wholly upon their wings for locomotion.

The rate of the wingbeats that in many species make a humming sound is difficult to determine, as it is far too rapid to be followed by the human eye. The most accurate counts have been made while the hummingbird was hovering rather than flying forward, by using a stroboscope in a darkened room. This apparatus emits extremely brief, bright flashes of light at exceedingly short intervals. If it is exactly synchronized with the wingbeats, they will always be illuminated in the same position, so that the bird will appear to float on motionless wings. The rate of the flashes can then be read on the instrument's dial. Using this method on a variety of hummingbirds, Scheithauer obtained frequencies of from twenty-two to seventy-nine wingbeats per second, the complete cycle of a down and up stroke being counted as one beat. The slowest rates were by the long-billed starthroat and the black-throated mango, large hummingbirds weighing respectively six and six and a half grams; the most rapid by the little white-bellied woodstar, which weighs only two and a half grams.

These results are in substantial agreement with those obtained earlier by C. H. Blake working with Harold Edgerton, by Crawford Greenewalt, and by other investigators. Just as a long pendulum swings more slowly than a short one, so a long wing beats more slowly than a short one. A mute swan's wing, twenty-eight inches long, flaps only one and a half times per second; a gnat's wing, a quarter of an inch in length, vibrates 500 times per second. Contrary to a prevalent impression, for their weight or wing length hummingbirds beat their wings less rather than more rapidly than other birds do. The giant hummingbird flaps only eight or ten times per second, whereas the much larger mockingbird does so about fourteen times. Many hummingbirds that weigh from five to seven grams flap at a rate of twenty to twenty-five times per second; but a chickadee, almost twice as heavy, beats its wings about twenty-seven times per second. Since only the chickadee's downstroke generates power, while both strokes of the hummingbird help to propel it, twenty-five beats of a hummingbird evidently count for fifty of the chickadee or some other "ordinary" bird. The hummingbird can afford to flap its wings more slowly because there is no wasted motion.

In courtship flights ruby-throated and rufous hummingbirds have been reported to beat their wings at the rate of 200 times per second.

At a given velocity, a small body appears to move faster than a large one—an optical illusion that is responsible for exaggerated claims of the speed of hummingbirds. A carefully controlled measurement of a hummingbird's velocity, made in a wind tunnel by Greenewalt, demonstrated that the top speed of a female rubythroat was 27 miles per hour. When the velocity of the air current passing through the tunnel was increased to 30 miles per hour, the bird tried vainly to reach the coveted syrup by flying against the current. Bees and wasps trying to reach the feeder in the same tunnel flew at a rate of scarcely more than 10 miles per hour. Augusto Ruschi observed flying speeds ranging from 14 to 25 miles per hour for several species of Brazilian hummingbirds on outdoor courses; he believed that none could exceed 30 miles per hour.

It appears, however, that under special conditions or with stronger motivation some kinds of hummingbirds can go faster. By taking motion pictures of an Allen's hummingbird diving earthward under wing power in courtship display, Oliver Pearson calculated its maximum velocity to be about 60 miles per hour. Using a stopwatch to time a male violet-ear's flight from one isolated tree to another, Helmuth Wagner found an average speed of over 56 miles per hour. In Scheithauer's indoor aviary, two long-tailed, or blue-throated, sylphs were in the habit of chasing each other, sometimes eight to twelve times without stopping, over a standard course, roughly a figure of eight, that led them through tropical vegetation and avoided enclosing walls. This course was about seventy-four yards long. By timing the birds repeatedly with a stopwatch, the aviculturist obtained velocities ranging from 30 to 47 miles per hour, with a mean of 38.4 miles per hour.

Although this speed may not impress people accustomed to jet travel, that a bird could hurtle so fast through obstructing vegetation in a small enclosed space, without dashing itself to death, reveals marvelously precise control of flight. And when we recall that songbirds, including those as large as thrushes, mostly fly at velocities between 20 and 35 miles per hour, and pigeons hardly go faster, the tiny hummingbird's performance commands admiration.

FROM *The Life of the Hummingbird*

Vision and Flight

CHARLTON OGBURN

In birds, flight and vision develop together. The swallow, which dips, twists, and turns in midair to catch small insects, the hawk that sees a mouse in a field from hundreds of feet above, the phoebe darting out from its perch after prey invisible to us, all need the superb sight they possess. The eyes of many species weigh more than their brains.

In the following passage from his book The Adventure of Birds, *Charlton Ogburn discusses the unique quality of a bird's eye.*

❧

Two other properties are essential for successful flight whether by living organisms or self-guiding missiles. There must be sensors capable of accurate, constant apprehension of what is ahead and a computer to receive the information and instantly instruct the guidance mechanism of needed changes in course. That birds are well endowed in both respects cannot be doubted by anyone who has seen them shoot swervingly through networks of branches or visualized nocturnal birds navigating and locating their prey in forests too dark to reveal the hand before the face to a human being. Robert Galambos and Donald R. Griffin of Harvard University, who discovered that bats guide themselves by "sonar"—emitting a series of high-pitched sounds and detecting objects in their path by the echo—have demonstrated that the cave-dwelling Oilbird, a distant relative of the Whip-poor-will's from northern South America, employs the same device. Since then a cave-nesting swift from the Philippines and Indonesia has been found to do likewise. The hearing of birds by human standards is preternaturally acute. A Barn Owl with eyes sealed can zero in on a mouse by its faint rustling in the leaves and strike it. And it is indicative of the refinement and novelty of adaptation that have gone into birds that the apertures of the ears of many owls are different in shape, the one on the right from the one on the left. The consequence must be to register the sound from the two sides in slightly unlike tones, and make for more accurate gauging of the direction of its source. But undoubtedly it is the light-gathering power of their eyes that chiefly serves the navigational needs of nocturnal birds. Owls' eyes, which may be as large as a human being's, are ten times or more as efficient in this as ours.

The quality of a bird's vision was brought home to me many years ago by a dwarf macaw I had as a pet and used to take for walks on my shoulder or wrist. Its attention would be riveted by an object approaching over the horizon before I could see anything at all. What was remarkable was that it would recognize the imperceptible dot as a hawk.

Any other kind of bird—a crow, for instance—it would ignore. Very often in winter today it will happen that the birds congregated around the house for the food we put out will suddenly disappear, except for a few caught at a distance from cover, and these will freeze. This is the sign of a Sharp-shinned or Cooper's Hawk in the vicinity. Whenever I notice this I go out to frighten off the intruder; but only *very* seldom can I see it.

There is no eye like a bird's eye. Change of focus in human vision depends on a muscle to contract and thicken the lens and on the natural resilience of the lens to restore it to its original shape. In birds there are muscles to do both jobs and others that change the shape of the cornea as well. They make possible an all-but-instantaneous shift in focus from sharp perception of objects at the limit of visibility to those a few beaks' lengths away. And a bird's perception is sharp indeed. Where the human eye has 200,000 visual cells per square millimeter in the place of greatest concentration in the retina—the fovea—G. L. Wall in his study of the vertebrate eye reports that these reach as high as one million in the European Buzzard (the equivalent of our Red-tailed Hawk), which he believes gives it a visual acuity at least eight times ours. On top of that a bird has two fovea. One is centrally located for lateral vision and quick detection of danger in any quarter, the other posteriorly for concentrated forward vision by the eyes together on an object for attack.

Birds' eyeballs are so large that they nearly meet at the septum. Adding musculature to move them would mean a larger skull and increased weight, and it has been dispensed with. Birds' eyes are fixed. The handicap, as it would be for us, is overcome in the great majority of birds by the placement of the eyes well back on the sides of the head. Here they command a nearly full field of view. A bird has almost all its surroundings under observation simultaneously and continuously, half with one eye, half with the other. It is not readily taken by surprise. The price is that there is not much overlap of the fields of vision of the two eyes. We see objects with both eyes together—that is, with binocular vision— through an arc amounting to about a quarter of a full circle, most birds through an arc only about a third as much. The Woodcock, which obtains its living by probing the mud for worms with its face close to the ground, has eyes so far up on its head and to the rear that it has wider binocular vision above it and behind than to the front—though not very wide anywhere. The habit of birds of cocking their heads is the corollary of monocular vision; they can best get a fix on an object with the direct stare of a single eye. The need to make certain demands more. As Louis Halle observes amusingly in a poignant account of the Adélie Penguin in *The Sea and the Ice,* "What is irresistibly comical, like the clown's smile, is the eye, one on each side of the pointed black face, which looks like a round white stone with a black disc in the middle, and the habit the penguin has of never trusting completely to either eye, so that, turning its head first this way and then that, it uses first one and then the other eye for a stare of apparent astonishment at the object to be observed." Owls are different. With forward-looking eyes and protruding corneas they have a complete overlap; everything they see, they see with both eyes. Because their field of vision is relatively narrow and their eyes immobile they are constantly swiveling their heads when on the alert; and they have the advantage of being able to look straight behind them. (All birds are compensated for their fixity of gaze by extreme suppleness of neck.) Hawks stand midway between owls and other birds in the placement and scope of their eyes.

An advantage of binocular, or stereoscopic vision, in movable eyes is in facilitating the gauging of distances; the eyes, working together, converge on close objects, the more so the closer, the less so the more distant. If you close one eye and reach out, quickly, to put a finger on a spot at arm's length you are apt to find that you miss it. In monocular vision distance must be judged by the diminution of the apparent size of an object with remoteness, by its position on an imaginary tape-measure laid out on the ground between the viewer and the horizon or by the difference between its apparent movement and that of other objects nearer and farther when the viewer, or at least his head, moves. (Children are fascinated to discover in a moving vehicle how objects on the horizon seem to be keeping pace with them—an illusion arising from the much faster apparent movement of objects in the foreground.) An owl's abrupt, rather ludicrous shifts of head from side to side while its gaze remains fixed on a target may have the purpose of exploiting this principle, as, it has been suggested, may the bobbing of heads by shorebirds. Whatever the correlations birds make to determine distance, they seem to do very well.

If the messages streaming from a bird's retina into the optic nerve are comprehensive and clear, its brain is well designed to handle them. To receive and classify the rapid fire of images there are large optic nerves, indicating a capacity for visual association—we are told—comparable with man's. The cerebellum is also large and well developed: it provides for precisely ordered responses to incoming stimuli of all kinds, automatically, instantaneously, through reflex action. A bird need not stop to think.

FROM *The Adventure of Birds*

Flight and Vision

J. A. BAKER

From J. A. Baker's fine book about the peregrine comes this description of this bird's superb vision, apparent during its hunting flights. In his writing, Baker succeeds at what many have tried and failed to do. Through constant, daily observations of the peregrine's movements in fine and exhaustive detail, he becomes keenly aware of such a bird's masterful alliance with the landscape it surveys.

The peregrine is adapted to the pursuit and killing of birds in flight. Its shape is streamlined. The rounded head and wide chest taper smoothly back to the narrow wedge-shaped tail. The wings are long and pointed; the primaries long and slender for speed, the secondaries long and broad to give strength for the lifting and carrying of heavy prey.

The hooked bill can pull flesh from bones. It has a tooth on the upper mandible, which fits into a notch in the lower one. This tooth can be inserted between the neck vertebrae of a bird so that, by pressing and twisting, the peregrine is able to snap the spinal cord. The legs are thick and muscular, the toes long and powerful. The toes have bumpy pads on their undersides that help in the gripping of prey. The bird-killing hind toe is the longest of the four, and it can be used separately for striking prey to the ground. The huge pectoral muscles give power and endurance in flight. The dark feathering around the eyes absorbs light and reduces glare. The contrasting facial pattern of brown and white may also have the effect of startling prey into sudden flight. To some extent it also camouflages the large, light-reflecting eyes.

The speed of the peregrine's wing-beat has been recorded as 4.4 beats per second. Comparative figures are: jackdaw 4.3, crow 4.2, lapwing 4.8, woodpigeon 5.2. In level flapping flight the peregrine looks rather pigeon-like, but its wings are longer and more flexible than a pigeon's and they curl higher above the back. The typical flight has been described as a succession of quick wing-beats, broken at regular intervals by long glides with wings extended. In fact, gliding is far from regular, and at least half the peregrine flights I have seen have contained few, if any, glides. When the hawk is not hunting, the flight may seem slow and undulating, but it is always faster than it looks. I have timed it at between thirty and forty miles an hour, and it is seldom less than that. Level pursuit of prey has reached speeds of fifty to sixty miles an hour over distances of a mile or more; speeds in excess of sixty m.p.h. were only attained for a much shorter time. The speed of the vertical stoop is undoubtedly well over a hundred miles an hour, but it is impossible to be more precise. The excitement of seeing a peregrine stoop cannot be defined by the use of statistics. . . . The eyes of a falcon peregrine weigh approximately one ounce each; they are larger and heavier than human eyes. If our eyes were in the same proportion to our bodies as the peregrine's are to his, a twelve stone man would have eyes three inches across, weighing four pounds. The whole retina of a hawk's eye records a resolution of distant objects that is twice as acute as that of the human retina. Where the lateral and binocular visions focus, there are deep-pitted foveal areas; their numerous cells record a resolution eight times as great as ours. This means that a hawk, endlessly scanning the landscape with small abrupt turns of his head, will pick up any point of movement; by focussing upon it he can immediately make it flare up into larger, clearer view.

The peregrine's view of the land is like the yachtsman's view of the shore as he sails into the long estuaries. A wake of water recedes behind him, the wake of the pierced horizon glides back on either side. Like the seafarer, the peregrine lives in a pouring-away world of no attachment, a world of wakes and tilting, of sinking planes of land and water. We who are anchored and earthbound cannot envisage this freedom of the eye. The peregrine sees and remembers patterns we do not know exist: the neat squares of orchard and woodland, the endlessly varying quadrilateral shapes of fields. He finds his way across the land by a succession of remembered symmetries. But what does he understand? Does he really 'know' that an object that increases in size is moving towards him? Or is it that he believes in the size he sees, so that a distant man is too small to be frightening but a man near is a man huge and therefore terrifying? He may live in a world of endless pulsations, of objects forever contracting or dilating in size. Aimed at a distant bird, a flutter of white wings, he may feel—as it spreads out beneath him like a stain of white— that he can never fail to strike. Everything he is has been evolved to link the targeting eye to the striking talon.

FROM *The Peregrine*

The Hunting Osprey

ALAN F. POOLE

The following passage describes the fishing techniques of the osprey, or fish hawk. Alan Poole's book Ospreys *is a landmark book for natural scientists, laymen, and students interested in this species. Poole, a graduate of the Yale School of Forestry and an early associate of Helen Hays, director of the American Museum's Great Gull Island program for nesting terns, is now the managing editor of* The Birds of North America, *a comprehensive series which will cover every bird species on the continent.*

☞

Most Ospreys hunt on the wing, actively searching out prey rather than quietly waiting at perches for fish to swim within striking distance. Flight burns about 10 times more energy than perching does, so the birds undoubtedly prefer to sit and wait for fish, although they can rarely do so efficiently. Even under ideal conditions—where lakes or streams have wooded shores, shallow margins, and a run of spawning fish—a perched bird can watch only a limited area. Thus it usually fares better on the wing, despite the extra cost. Wintering birds tend to perch-hunt more than breeders do, perhaps because they have only themselves to feed and so can afford to wait longer for each fish caught.

Although it is difficult to tell when a perched Osprey is actually hunting, it is obvious with birds on the wing. Instead of rowing along in direct flight, fishing Ospreys fly slowly, sometimes circling back on themselves and often pulling up briefly to hover before moving on again, apparently stalking their prey. No one knows exactly what stimulates a hover. Hovering birds constantly scan the waters below, so spotting a fish or just seeing likely habitat could prompt this action.

The dive itself is spectacular, a quick release of tension built up during the preceding minutes. A diving Osprey tucks back its wings and abandons itself to the pull of gravity, usually falling steeply but maneuvering subtly with wing and tail all the while, to keep on track toward its target. If unsure about a fish, the hawk may drop down in gradual steps for a closer look before making its final plunge or veering off to another area. Dives are sometimes aborted before hitting the water, the bird swooping up at the last moment if its prey proves elusive or undesirable.

Try landing a fish 15%–30% of your own weight with your bare hands and you will begin to appreciate the problems of an Osprey lifting its struggling prey from the water. Even if the bird's talons strike deep, most fish are tough, die slowly, and struggle violently. To combat this, Ospreys often rest briefly on the water after diving, probably securing their prey, and then reach high with long, fast, almost horizontal wing strokes that start well above the tail and sweep down and forward of the head to eye level. The birds seem to gain much of their lift with the outer tips of their wings, taking off slowly like helicopters with heavy payloads. Once airborne, an Osprey usually rearranges its prey, one foot ahead of the other, so the fish's head points forward and its body is tucked close to the bird. This cuts wind resistance and speeds flight back to nest or perch. Most Ospreys fly low when bucking strong headwinds, hugging the surface of land or water and avoiding the worst blasts by doing so. If wet from diving, the hawks nearly always shake off in midair, twisting rapidly from head to tail and looking for all the world like a wet dog drying off after a swim.

Ospreys do most of their hunting five to 40 meters above the water, but this and other aspects of foraging behavior vary with the fish pursued. When hunting fast-moving surface fish like mullet and herring, for example, the birds often fly close to the water, diving at low angles without hovering or fluttering down to snatch fish from the surface, barely wetting their legs. In Senegal, by contrast, Prevost watched Ospreys circle up high, 100–300 meters above the water, when searching for schools of sardines (*Sardinella* spp.) and flying fish (*Cheilopogon* spp.) several kilometers offshore. After spotting a school, the birds dropped down again before diving. Such offshore fishing is unusual for Ospreys, but it shows how alert they are to the sudden appearance of fish. Most often, hunting Ospreys hug coastlines or follow streams, venturing out only over small bays, lakes, and inlets.

Ospreys usually hunt alone, but small groups will form where food is especially plentiful. On Florida Bay, I have watched these birds, six or eight at a time, hovering together over schools of mullet that Porpoises (*Tursiops truncatus*) had driven into shallow water. Brown Pelicans (*Pelicanus occidentalis*) and various gulls often joined the diving melee, a pleasing kaleidoscope of mammal, bird, and fish that might have adorned a Greek vase centuries ago.

FROM *Ospreys*

Wideawake Fair

ROBERT CUSHMAN MURPHY

The following account of a colony of sooty terns is taken from
Oceanic Birds of South America *by Robert Cushman Mur-*
phy (1887–1973), onetime head of the Department of Orni-
thology at the American Museum of Natural History in New
York. The sooty tern is a black and white bird that breeds on
tropical islands from the Atlantic to the Pacific. Otherwise, it
spends much of its life on the wing, soaring at great heights on
the lookout for its food. Seen from a distance, "they hang like
canopies of smoke above their breeding grounds."

This famous colony of sooties, on Ascension Island in the
mid-south Atlantic, is called "Wideawake Fair" because of the
constant clamor of its population, night and day.

⤳

The site is well sheltered from wind by the hills and is very
oppressive under the full blaze of the tropical sun, the more

so because of an overpowering odor that arises from it during the time that the birds are present. The stench comes not alone from guano, but also from dead bodies of young and adults and innumerable cracked or addled eggs, among which carrion beetles and their larvae swarm. From the slopes of Green Mountain one can see the area as a greenish white patch, looking as though the bed of cinders had been whitened by a light fall of snow, while in the air above the wheeling and hovering terns appear like a pillar of cloud that is never dissipated during the hours of daylight. The tremendous noise, which is so discordant and ear-splitting at close range, blends in the distance to a sound like the murmuring of a vast crowd of human beings.

Besides the special aggregation at Wideawake Fair, there are or formerly were several lesser colonies at Ascension, as well as one on the flat-topped adjacent islet known as Boatswain-bird. The terns of these separate rookeries arrive and depart with those of the Fair, and all observers agree that, on the average, the nesting season begins about three months earlier each successive year, so that instead of nesting once a year the Sooty Terns breed about four times in each three-year period. Wilkins puts the fact in other words when he states that they return to nest about once every nine months. . . . At sunrise the Sooty Terns are spontaneously most noisy. The individual notes have been likened to a sharp staccato laugh, with which longer, more musical tones are occasionally mingled. Soon after the break of day, the free birds leave their island in search of breakfast, often mingling, purely from a community of interest, with noddies, boobies, and other sea fowl over the ocean. They feed without plunging or in any other way touching the water. They capture their food rather by pursuing shoals of small fish, such as herrings and carangids, and doubtless larval

flying fish, and deftly picking these out of the air as they
leap above the surface. After sufficiently gorging themselves, the Sooties spend much time in sheer aërial maneu-
vers, and sometimes join the frigate-birds in soaring higher
and higher until they are lost to sight.

FROM *The Oceanic Birds of South America*

Playing with the Wind

KONRAD LORENZ

Konrad Lorenz, a lifelong student of animal behavior, was a pioneer in the science of ethnology. As this extract about jackdaws from King Solomon's Ring *shows, his feeling of companionship for the animals he studied gave his work an unusual warmth and depth of perception.*

⟡

In the chimney the autumn wind sings the song of the elements, and the old firs before my study window wave excitedly with their arms and sing so loudly in chorus that I can hear their sighing melody through the double panes. Suddenly, from above, a dozen black, streamlined projectiles shoot across the piece of clouded sky for which my window forms a frame. Heavily as stones they fall, fall to the tops of the firs where they suddenly sprout wings, become birds and then light feather rags that the storm seizes

and whirls out of my line of vision, more rapidly than they
were borne into it.

I walk to the window to watch this extraordinary game
that the jackdaws are playing with the wind. A game? Yes,
indeed, it is a game, in the most literal sense of the word:
practised movements, indulged in and enjoyed for their
own sake and not for the achievement of a special object.
And rest assured, these are not merely inborn, purely instinctive actions, but movements that have been carefully
learned. All these feats that the birds are performing, their
wonderful exploitation of the wind, their amazingly exact
assessment of distances and, above all, their understanding
of local wind conditions, their knowledge of all the upcur-
rents, air pockets and eddies—all this proficiency is no in-
heritance, but, for each bird, an individually acquired
accomplishment.

And look what they do with the wind! At first sight, you,
poor human being, think that the storm is playing with the
birds, like a cat with a mouse, but soon you see, with astonishment, that it is the fury of the elements that here plays
the role of the mouse and that the jackdaws are treating the
storm exactly as the cat its unfortunate victim. Nearly, but
only nearly, do they give the storm its head, let it throw
them high, high into the heavens, till they seem to fall upwards, then, with a casual flap of a wing, they turn themselves over, open their pinions for a fraction of a second
from below against the wind, and dive—with an acceler-
ation far greater than that of a falling stone—into the
depths below. Another tiny jerk of the wing and they return
to their normal position and, on close-reefed sails, shoot
away with breathless speed into the teeth of the gale, hundreds of yards to the west: this all playfully and without
effort, just to spite the stupid wind that tries to drive them

towards the east. The sightless monster itself must perform the work of propelling the birds through the air at a rate of well over 80 miles an hour; the jackdaws do nothing to help beyond a few lazy adjustments of their black wings. Sovereign control over the power of the elements, intoxicating triumph of the living organism over the pitiless strength of the inorganic!

FROM *King Solomon's Ring*

The Wandering Albatross

PABLO NERUDA

The wind sails the open sea
steered by the albatross
that glides, falls, dances, climbs,
hangs motionless in the fading light,
touches the waves' towers,
settles down in
the disorderly element's
seething mortar
while the salt crowns it with laurels
and the furious foam hisses,
skims the waves
with its great symphonic wings,
leaving above the tempest
a book that flies on forever:
the statute of the wind.

FROM *Art of the Birds* (Jack Schmitt, tr.)

Part Two

The Language
of Birds

European literature gives the impression that either the lark
or the nightingale was the principal singing bird. So, from
Shakespeare's *Cymbeline:* "Hark! hark! the lark at heaven's
gate sings," or from *Romeo and Juliet*:

> It was the nightingale, and not the lark,
> That pierc'd the fearful hollow of thine ear;
> Nightly she sings on yon pomegranate tree.

In North America, some would argue, the songs of the
hermit thrush or the wood thrush are superior to those of
these Old World birds. Apart from what we hear as inspir-
ingly musical, of course, lies a wide range of vocalization,
including sounds that vary from the high, rasping scream
of a red-tailed hawk hovering in the air to the sharp-edged
kip of a sanderling hurrying along the tideline. Bird voices
can sound like a flute or, as with the bittern, a pile-driver
in a swamp. The bell bird at the edge of a clearing in the

rainforest clangs like a metal pipe hit with a hammer. Singing during courtship or territorial displays represents an intensification of feeling. A few species, like the famous skylark, engage in flight singing, performed as they rise high in the air above the ground.

Just as there are many distinct species, there are many different calls birds make. Sometimes their calls signal new sources of food; sometimes they warn of outside aggression; or, they may relate to courtship behavior or simply reflect "family talk" at the nest.

The voices of the gulls cry out above the wind, conveying their thousands of years of association with the shores of the globe. The song of the waterthrush complements the streams and waterfalls it inhabits. The flutelike notes of the hermit thrush roll down the aisles formed by forest trees. The intonations and echoes of bird calls vary according to the terrain they fly through. They reflect the subtle interactions of the worlds they inhabit. The earth speaks through the birds not with the rigidity and literalism through which we are inclined to judge them, but out of its endless fund of spontaneous expression.

In order to distinguish human speech from the calls of birds, we refer to their "vocalizing," and their "communication." But what are they communicating? Messages, for one thing, expressing basic needs and intentions. Birds are emotional creatures, and so they signal sudden feelings of alarm or aggression. In what we hear as a kind of abbreviated dialogue, their calls indicate inner pressures and necessities which follow out of their lives. Completely engaged in the business of living, birds do not and cannot spend time on consciously thinking about the alternatives to what they do.

Birds and the Flute: The Pipes of Pan

LUCRETIUS

The music of the flute has followed and been inspired by the songs of birds over thousands of years. Few wooden instruments survive the weathering of time, but some flutes made of the hollow bones of birds, reindeer, and bear have been found in Ice Age caves, dating back to between 20,000 and 30,000 years ago. They were certainly well known in Graeco-Roman times, as shown in this extract from De Rerum Natura, *or* On Nature, *by the Roman poet and philosopher Lucretius, 96–55 B.C.*

✦

Men imitated the voices of birds with their own lips long before they were able to practice polished songs and give pleasure to the ear. The whispering of the breeze through the hollow reeds first taught farmers to blow upon the

pipes of Pan. Then little by little they learned the sweet laments that, when stopped by the fingers of the player, the
pipe pours forth, an instrument developed among pathless
groves and woods and pastures in the charming and solitary
spots where shepherds rest. They soothed and delighted
their hearts with such music when they were filled with
food, for then anything pleases. Thus as they lay in groups
on the soft grass beside a stream of water beneath the
branches of a tall tree, they often found comfort for their
bodies in simple ways, especially when the weather was
pleasant and the season of the year painted with flowers
the grass as it grew green. Then jokes, conversation, and
pleasant laughter were the rule; then was the rustic Muse
at her best; then happy Mirth taught them to bind heads
and shoulders with wreaths woven of flowers and leaves.
Then moving their limbs without rhythm they advanced in
rude dance, rudely striking with their feet the earth, their
mother. From this there arose jests and pleasant laughter,
since all this, being new and therefore more worthy of wonder, was then in favor. For those forced to remain awake,
these were the solaces for the lack of sleep: to sing in various
ways as they followed the melody, and to run the hooked
lip along the pipes. Hence even now watchmen accept these
songs as traditional and learn to sing in rhythm; and they
do not enjoy any greater sweetness than did the woodland
race of the earth-born.

FROM *De Rerum Natura* (Russell M. Geer, tr.)

Kokopelli:
Symbol of a Continent
of Birds

TERRY TEMPEST WILLIAMS

Among Native Americans, the legend of the humpbacked flute player was widespread for many thousands of years. Pictographs of him have been found on rocks all the way from southern South America to Canada. Kokopelli, as he was called, used to play his flute while he accompanied people on their migrations. In the hump on his back he carried the seeds of flowering plants which he would scatter at intervals on the ground. Kokopelli sang a song as he went, which is so old, according to some anthropologists, that its meaning has been completely lost. Perhaps we can hear him still, in some canyon of the West, as Terry Tempest Williams suggests.

⤳

One night, beneath the ruins of Keet Seel, we heard flute music—music so sweet it could have split the seeds of corn. Earlier we had wandered through the rooms of Keet Seel, admiring the redrock construction dabbed into the sandstone alcove like swallows' nests, but there had been no music then—only the silence pressing against us in the cool Anasazi air.

Above the ruins, clouds covered the full face of the moon like gauze. The land seemed to bow with the melody of the flute. I reached for my husband's arm and he reached for our friend. We kept hold of one another like children, and we listened, holding our breaths between the intervals of our own heartbeats. The flute music flowed out from the cliff dwelling like an ancient breath.

The next morning we sat around camp, drinking rose hip tea. We were tired and stiff from the cold, still half stunned from the night before. Our friend, who was Hopi, looked down at the cup he held in both hands, and told a story.

A man traveled through this country with a bag of corn seed over one shoulder. His shadow against the desert looked like a deformity. He would stop at every village and teach the people how to plant corn. And then when the sun slipped behind the mesa and the village was asleep, he would walk through the cornfields playing his flute. The seeds would flower, pushing themselves up through the red, sandy soil and follow the high-pitched notes upward. The sun would rise and the man would be gone, with corn stalks the height of a young girl shimmering in the morning light. Many of the young women would complain of a fullness in their bellies. The elders would smile, knowing they were pregnant. They would look to the southwest and call him "Kokopelli."

We finished our tea, broke up our camp, and organized our packs for the trail. Before leaving, I walked back to the base of Keet Seel. The ruins appeared darker than usual, full of shadows that moved from room to room. My eyes followed the tall timbers from floor to ceiling as I imagined macaws perched on top. Kivas held darkness below, and I wondered if old men's bones might be buried there. Just then, in a stream of light, a pictograph on the ceiling of the alcove jumped out. It was a buglike creature, but as I focused more clearly I recognized it as the humpbacked flute player.

"Kokopelli," I whispered to myself. "It must be Kokopelli."

The light shifted and he seemed to be rocking on his back. I had missed him the day before, noticing only the pictographs of bighorn sheep and spirals. At that moment, I recalled the flute music that flooded the canyon the night before and the clouds like gossamer hands with long, long fingers that pulled me into an abyss of sleep. I placed my hand over my stomach, turned away from the ruins, and walked back toward my fellow campers. Halfway down the canyon, I felt stirrings in my belly. Sweet corn was sprouting all along the river.

FROM *Coyote Canyon*

Bird Song

KARL RASMUSSEN

What we hear when we listen to the calls and songs of the birds depends in large part on our culture. Those influenced by science may refer to such sounds as vocalizing, or communicating. Others are inclined to think of bird song as an automatic reaction. So birds are dismissed or trivialized, though we may enjoy hearing the first robin in the spring.

What birds are "saying" is unclear, though we know them as emotional creatures, whose songs and calls reflect basic moods and necessities. Our confusion may have much to do with the modern attitude toward what we abstractly refer to as the "environment," whose plants and animals often seem to exist in name only. In the first poem that follows there is no such division. With magic words, the human tongue replicates the sounds of birds and addresses their spirits. It encompasses the

spontaneity rising from the cry of a gull and the heart of a human being sharing the same world. The second poem tells what
the first one shows.

The great gull hovers
on wings spread wide
above us, above us.
He stares, I shout!
His head is white,
his beak gapes,
his small round eyes
look far, look sharp!
      Qutiuk! Qutiuk!

The great skua hovers
on wings spread wide
above us, above us.
He stares, I shout!
His head is black,
his beak gapes,
his small round eyes
look far, look sharp!
      Ijoq! Ijoq!

The great raven hovers
on wings spread wide
above us, above us.
He stares, I shout!
His head is blue-black,
his beak is sharp

(does it have teeth?)
His eyes squint!
   Qara! Qara!

And then there is the owl,
the great owl!
He hovers
on wings spread wide
above us, above us.
He stares, I shout!
His head is swollen,
his beak is hooked,
and his round eyes
have lids turned inside out,
red and heavy!
   Oroq! Oroq!

FROM *Eskimo Poems*

Magic Words

KARL RASMUSSEN

In the very earliest time,
when both people and animals lived on earth,
a person could become an animal if he wanted to
and an animal could become a human being.
Sometimes they were people
and sometimes animals
and there was no difference.
All spoke the same language.
That was the time when words were like magic.
The human mind had mysterious powers.
A word spoken by chance
might have strange consequences.
It would suddenly come alive
and what people wanted to happen could happen.
All you had to do was say it.
Nobody could explain this,
that's the way it was.

FROM *Eskimo Songs and Stories*

The Loon

RICHARD K. NELSON

As Richard K. Nelson points out in his book Make Prayers to the Raven, *the Koyukons of Alaska "seem to conceptualize humans and animals as very similar beings. This derives not so much from the animal nature of humans as from the human nature of animals." Accordingly, each species has its own spirit that should not be mistreated and offended. Men, women, and children observe time-honored rules of behavior toward the loon and other creatures, part of the courtesy of a common existence in the subarctic world. It is not surprising that the people should revere that great voice of the wilderness, the voice of the loon.*

I will begin with the common loon (*Gavia immer*), a bird whose English name is somewhat inappropriate for interior

Alaska, where it certainly is not abundant; nor by anyone's standards could it be judged ordinary. Common loons are very large birds, strikingly marked with a geometric design in black and white. According to stories of the Distant Time, the man who became *dodzina,* the common loon, used his medicine to restore another man's sight. In return he was given a cape with elaborate dentalium-shell decorations (dentalium shells formerly reached interior Alaska through trade networks), and its pattern remains on the loon's back and neck.

Koyukon people so admire and appreciate this bird that they sometimes keep its stuffed skin as an object of beauty. The entire skin, with head and beak intact, is filled with dried grass, and often it is hung inside the house where people can always see it. Other birds and animals are also kept this way, either for aesthetic reasons or for good luck. One family in Huslia had a red-throated loon, snow bunting, harlequin duck, bufflehead, flicker, and least and short-tailed weasels hung in the main room of their house. The flicker and weasels were also elaborately decorated with jewelry trinkets.

The common loon is even more remarkable for its voice—a completely indescribable arrangement of high-pitched falsetto cries, long wailing laments, and eerie laughter. Heard at evening in the silent wildlands, from the shore of a lake surrounded by deep timber, it is the essence and beauty of the north country itself. The Koyukon people express great appreciation for the loon's call, not only because of its resplendent sound but also because it manifests the animal's considerable spirit powers.

Traditionally the elders have listened to the loon as a source of inspiration in composing their own songs. An old man from Hughes once tried to explain to me just how important and powerful this inspiration is. He told me a Koyukon saying, then gave a figurative translation to impart its full meaning and substance in English:

> When a loon calls on a lake, it is the greatest voice that a human can hear. [Ots'aa dodzin tongheedo beeznee eene-e'ʌon; literally, "The loon's call is the one against which all others are judged."]

This man showed a remarkable gift for seeing nature in special ways, and no animal seemed to impress him more deeply than the loon. Its compelling personality fascinated him and inspired his respect. Once he told me, at great length and with powerful words that came much faster than I could write exactly, about the loon's first arrival in spring:

> Loons always come in after good weather turns cloudy and rainy, around breakup time. If you happen to be in the right place, at just the right time, you might hear a rushing sound coming from way up high above. Then if you look quickly and can see well, you might see a loon diving right down, headlong from the sky, with its wings folded back, coming straight toward that lake. At the very last moment, the loon will swoop up and fly level at great speed just over the water. Then it will make a long skim on the surface, finally stop, and dive down underneath.
>
> A minute later you'll see it bob up; and listen, you'll hear it make a short cry, soft . . . it's letting everything know, it's announcing: "Here I am!" That's the loon when it gets here for the first time in spring.

Stories of the Distant Time say that Koyukon songs originated partly from the loon's crying and partly from the human imagination. Perhaps this too is why loon calls are especially meaningful. After the late elder, Chief Henry, passed away, I was sitting near his house with an old man from Allakaket. "It would be good to hear *dodzina* [the loon] right now," he said quietly. "We really like to hear that music." He had tears in his eyes as he talked about that beautiful wild voice, about hunters listening to it as they paddle their canoes from lake to lake in the spring. And he seemed to wish for it now as a good sign or a gift from the natural world to the spirit of a great hunter. I could scarcely have troubled him to explain further.

A few days earlier, while Chief Henry lay near death, an old woman from a Yukon village walked to the nearby shore of *Binkookk'a* Lake. She stood at the water's edge and sang Koyukon "spring songs" to a pair of loons that had been in the lake for several weeks. Shortly, the loons swam toward her until they rested in the water some fifty yards away, and there they answered her, filling the air with eerie and wonderful voices. When I spoke with her later, she said that loons will often answer spring songs this way. For several days people talked of how beautiful the exchange of songs had been that morning.

Loons can give signs in several different ways. If someone walks up to a lakeshore and a loon in the water dives immediately with an abrupt, alarmed note, it is a very bad sign. Done repeatedly, it foretells serious illness or death for the person or a close relative. A certain long, wailing cry, on the other hand, means that an animal is nearby, often a bear. A loon flying upstream low over the water, giving short wavering calls, is foretelling rainy weather. And a person can expect good luck if he sees a pair of loons running toward him across the water, bodies erect and wings cocked peculiarly behind them.

Common loons are rarely eaten, and then only by elders who need not fear becoming awkward and slow. In times of food shortage, however, people would hunt birds like this, preferring to risk clumsiness rather than starvation. The loon's eggs are never eaten, because disturbing its nest will cause a heavy wind.

> Sometimes people will hunt the loon, but me, I don't like to kill it. I like to listen to it all I can and pick up the words it knows.

The yellow-billed loon (*Gavia adamsii*) is nearly identical to the common loon in size, voice, and behavior. It also looks the same, except that its bill is creamy rather than black and is slightly different in shape. According to one very knowledgeable man, these two loons are actually varieties of one form in the Koyukon conception. But the yellow-billed loon (*dodibeeya*) is more powerful. It makes the same signs, but they are more significant. And "it says the same words, but its voice is just a little different." A person who kills one and keeps its skin will have a lifetime of good luck afterward; but they are extremely rare, so taking one is nearly unheard of. An elder from Hughes told me that he knew of only three people who had ever succeeded.

The Arctic loon (*Gavia arctica*) is a similar-looking but smaller bird, with a frost of white on its head. Its Koyukon name *tl'idlibaa,* was translated by one person (perhaps rather imaginatively) as "active in the water." It is said to be very quick, "almost like an otter," so it is difficult to shoot. Only old people are permitted to eat it, and like the other loons its skin is sometimes stuffed and kept for its beauty.

The red-throated loon (*Gavia stellata*), like the Arctic loon, is not accorded special power or significance in Koyukon culture. It is called *tokootsaagha,* "cries into the water," and people rarely hunt or eat it. Only the meat of loons or grebes is used for food, not the head, feet, or viscera. People occasionally also use feathered skins to make covered cushions, taking advantage of their natural designs.

FROM *Make Prayers to the Raven*

Thoreau and the Birds

HENRY DAVID THOREAU

Unlike participants in modern natural history field trips, who are usually concerned with finding the correct names of whatever natural objects they meet, Henry David Thoreau was not the type to travel in groups, nose in a field guide. It is hard to imagine Thoreau on any sort of field trip. Although he might take walks with a friend, he was not inclined to follow anyone's lead but his own. His real leaders were the woodlands, the fields, and the rivers, and they led him far beyond his native Concord. The birds provided him with a music that extended past their names.

❧

Bluejays and Chickadees

DECEMBER 31, 1850: The blue jays evidently notify each other of the presence of an intruder, and will sometimes make a great chattering about it, and so communicate the alarm to other birds and to beasts.

JULY 8, 1852: The jay's note, resounding along a raw woodside, suggests a singular wildness.

FEBRUARY 2, 1854: The scream of the jay is a true winter sound. It is wholly without sentiment, and in harmony with winter. I stole up within five or six feet of a pitch pine behind which a downy woodpecker was pecking. From time to time he hopped round to the side and observed me without fear. They are very confident birds, not easily scared, but incline to keep the other side of the bough to you, perhaps.

FEBRUARY 12, 1854: You hear the lisping tinkle of chickadees from time to time and the unrelenting steel-cold scream of a jay, unmelted, that never flows into a song, a sort of wintry trumpet, screaming cold; hard, tense, frozen music, like the winter sky itself; in the blue livery of winter's band. It is like a flourish of trumpets to the winter sky. There is no hint of incubation in the jay's scream. Like the creak of a cart-wheel.

Wood thrush

JUNE 14, 1853: The wood thrush launches forth his evening strains from the midst of the pines. I admire the moderation of this master. There is nothing tumultuous in his song. He launches forth one strain with all his heart and life and soul, of pure and unmatchable melody, and then he pauses and gives the hearer and himself time to digest this, and then another and another at suitable intervals. Men talk of the *rich* song of other birds—the thrasher, mockingbird, nightingale. But I doubt, I doubt. They know not what they say! There is as great an interval between the thrasher and the wood thrush as between Thomson's *Sea-*

sons and Homer. The sweetness of the day crystallizes in
the morning coolness.

JUNE 22, 1853: As I come over the hill, I hear the wood
thrush singing his evening lay. This is the only bird whose
note affects me like music, affects the flow and tenor of my
thought, my fancy and imagination. It lifts and exhilarates
me. It is inspiring. It is a medicative draught to my soul. It
is an elixir to my eyes and a fountain of youth to all my
senses. It changes all hours to an eternal morning. It ban-
ishes all trivialness. It reinstates me in my dominion, makes
me the lord of creation, is chief musician of my court. This
minstrel sings in a time, a heroic age, with which no event
in the village can be contemporary. How can they be contemporary when only the latter is *temporary* at all? How
can the infinite and eternal be contemporary with the finite
and temporal? So there is something in the music of the
cow-bell, something sweeter and more nutritious, than in
the milk which the farmers drink. This thrush's song is a
ranz des vaches to me. I long for wildness, a nature which I
cannot put my foot through, woods where the wood thrush
forever sings, where the hours are early morning ones, and
there is dew on the grass, and the day is forever unproved,
where I might have a fertile unknown for a soil about me.
I would go after the cows, I would watch the flocks of Ad-
metus there forever, only for my board and clothes. A New
Hampshire everlasting and unfallen.

Sparrow

MAY 1897: If you would hear the song of the sparrow inside you a thousand years hence, let your life be in harmony
with its strains today.

FROM *Thoreau on Birds* and
The Journals of Henry David Thoreau

Almanac

DONALD CULROSS PEATTIE

*Donald Culross Peattie was a natural scientist, trained in bot-
any as well as entomology. As a professional botanist, he wrote
numerous books and papers, and he was once honored for his
poetry.* An Almanac for Moderns, *a rare blend of poetry and
natural science published in 1935, encouraged many readers in
their love of the American land.*

MAY 11: A day of silver rain, pouring down straight and
tumultuously on the roofs, on the trees; silver rain like a
flight of javelins blown down from all over the sky. And the
white-throat singing, perhaps for the last time before this
little winter resident takes flight. Some say he sings of
"Sweet Canada, Can-a-da, Can-a-da!" where he goes to
mate, but to me he seems to cry "Oh, long ago, long ago,
long ago!"

Compared to him the vaunting skylark of the poets does no more than twitter. The meadowlark is like the eery happy whistle of the wind through the grass in the time when Queen Anne's lace bobs in the fields of blue June, and the thrush is the voice of serenity, of green twilights in very lonely hushed woods, a singer who makes a cathedral wherever he lifts his voice.

But the white-throat's touching chromatic pierces the heart; it blends sadness and happiness in a way to catch the listener in either mood, and the only other bird song to which it can be compared is that of the nightingale. Their songs are physically alike in the delicate chromatic of the notes, the purity of the tone, and the way that they let their voices swell upon a note until the tears start in the eyes of the listener. The white-throat, too, has a song like a cry, a song that speaks of the antiquity of time, the briefness of life.

JUNE 30: As a child I did not dream that our meadowlarks were not the skylarks of the poets in whose books my elder sister read. Lord Fairfax, as he sailed up the Rappahannock, released the English skylarks into the hostile New World. There is recurrent a legend around Fredericksburg that skylarks still persist. The skylark has accidentally reached Bermuda, and was once introduced around New York, but has unfortunately failed to establish itself as the domestic sparrow and starling have done. Apparently it is necessary to have some objectionable features in order to get on in this world.

Our only real larks are the horned larks that sometimes come to us in winter. But to what a merry family do our meadowlarks belong, that numbers within its fold the orioles, the grackles, the bobolinks and redwinged blackbirds, a wholly New World family, of which every member known to me has black in the plumage, just enough of it to be smart and jaunty, combined as it is with orange and yellow, and, in the case of the grackles, with green and purple highlights.

At this moment the meadowlarks whistle good-by to June; *ss-wheee-tu-yu,* they call across the meadow where abandoned old apple trunks, orchard grass and Queen Anne's lace all lean one way. Their voices call from the north, and, like an echo, against the hills from the south, but ever out of sight, until the whole blue basin of heaven is ringing with their cries. Though the song bubbles upward from the grass, it sounds as though it fell from the faultless blue of the sky.

FROM *An Almanac for Moderns*

Mimicry

ROGER J. PASQUIER

The following is taken from Watching Birds, *a highly readable and instructive book on the behavior and characteristics of birds. The author, Roger Pasquier, is currently engaged in an effort to conserve and protect tropical species.*

There seems to be little agreement on the function of mimicry, the remarkable ability of some birds to imitate the songs and calls of others as well as the intonations of human speech, and particular sounds that may intrigue them.

In this country, the group of birds called the Mimidae *includes mockingbird, catbird, and brown thrasher. One mockingbird, which deserved the title champion, was heard imitating fifty-nine other species of birds during the course of an hour.*

———

Vocal mimicry, the ability to imitate sounds one has heard, is limited to birds and humans. It is one of the indications that sound production is not just an inherited, purely instinctive ability; birds, like people, are capable of learning new ways of operating the mechanisms that produce sounds.

Mimicry is found in several passerine families, in parrots, and in cuckoos. In most cases its function is still unknown. Mimics are found in habitats from bare open ground to dense scrub to forest; some mimic while in flight, others from the ground or a concealed or exposed perch. This variety makes it difficult to suggest ecological reasons why the ability to mimic is advantageous.

North America's ablest and best known mimic is the Mockingbird. Other members of its family, the Brown Thrasher and Gray Catbird, for example, are also good mimics, as are crows, jays, and Starlings. All are able to imitate other bird calls and songs, animal sounds, and mechanical sounds. Some can reproduce a sound as soon as they hear it, others must hear a sound several times. Most mimics are stimulated by the sounds they hear. In spring a Mockingbird will reproduce the songs of returning migrants as soon as they arrive; at the end of the spring it sings many more songs than early in the season. The Mockingbird may continue to sing songs of birds that have departed or ceased singing themselves. Captive Mockingbirds may reproduce sounds years after they last heard them. Like other mimics, the Mockingbird is sometimes stimulated to mimic a particular sound when it sees the bird or object which makes it. While the Mockingbird seems to reproduce other birds' songs very accurately, the other species are not fooled, perhaps because the Mockingbird sings so many different songs in succession; it would be an inconvenience, not an advantage, to any mimic if it actually fooled other birds.

"Talking" birds—those that can imitate human speech —are less common than mimics. The Gray Parrot of Africa is considered the best talker, but many other parrots, as well as mynahs, magpies, and crows, are able talkers. The European Robin and the European Blackbird, a thrush in the same genus as the American Robin, have occasionally learned to mimic human speech. It is curious that in the wild the vocabulary of most parrots is limited to raucous shrieks; that they imitate no sounds in the wild seems to indicate that the ability has no adaptive significance.

Talking birds do not really understand the meaning of what they say and cannot put together sentences they have not heard spoken, even if they have used in other phrases all the words needed for that sentence. Some birds, parrots especially, have remarkable powers of association and will say "good-bye" if they see someone leaving or, occasionally, someone they don't like arriving. Parrots may also repeat a phrase only when the appropriate person is present. One Gray Parrot could whistle music by Beethoven when only the name of the piece was mentioned.

Vocal mimicry has evolved twice to serve an important biological function. In Africa and India, species of cuckoos and indigobirds (in the family of the House Sparrow) that lay their eggs in the nests of other birds, which will raise the young as their own, have calls that mimic their host species. The young of a cuckoo called the Koel has begging notes like those of its usual nestmates—Indian Crows. The young Koel evidently learns to imitate calls by hearing them; Koels raised without Indian Crows do not use their call. Indigobirds include the song of their usual host in their own; the imitative song of the male indigobird may draw the host female away from the nest so that the female in-digobird can deposit her egg. As each male mimics the song of only one of the species' several hosts, this may help fe-male indigobirds recognize appropriate mates, since each lays eggs in the nests of only one species.

FROM *Watching Birds*

Spring

ANNIE DILLARD

Annie Dillard asks fanciful and appealing questions of the kind that often occur to those who stop to listen to birds. Why do birds sing? What are they saying? Their open-ended and elusive songs, calls, or conversations elude us, challenging the sense of our own speech and the sensibility behind it.

When I was quite young I fondly imagined that all foreign languages were codes for English. I thought that "hat," say, was the real and actual name of the thing, but that people in other countries, who obstinately persisted in speaking the code of their forefathers, might use the word "ibu," say, to designate not merely the concept hat, but the English *word* "hat." I knew only one foreign word, "oui," and since it had three letters as did the word for which it was a code, it seemed, touchingly enough, to confirm my theory. Each

foreign language was a different code, I figured, and at
school I would eventually be given the keys to unlock some
of the most important codes' systems. Of course I knew that
it might take years before I became so fluent in another language that I could code and decode easily in my head, and
make of gibberish a nimble sense. On the first day of my
first French course, however, things rapidly took on an entirely unexpected shape. I realized that I was going to have
to learn speech all over again, word by word, one word at
a time—and my dismay knew no bounds.

The birds have started singing in the valley. Their February squawks and naked chirps are fully fledged now, and
long lyrics fly in the air. Birdsong catches in the mountains'
rim and pools in the valley; it threads through forests, it
slides down creeks. At the house a wonderful thing happens. The mockingbird that nests each year in the front-
yard spruce strikes up his chant in high places, and one of
those high places is my chimney. When he sings there, the
hollow chimney acts as a soundbox, like the careful emptiness inside a cello or violin, and the notes of the song
gather fullness and reverberate through the house. He sings
a phrase and repeats it exactly; then he sings another and
repeats that, then another. The mockingbird's invention is
limitless; he strews newness about as casually as a god. He
is tireless, too; toward June he will begin his daily marathon
at two in the morning and scarcely pause for breath until
eleven at night. I don't know when he sleeps.

When I lose interest in a given bird, I try to renew it by
looking at the bird in either of two ways. I imagine neu-
trinos passing through its feathers and into its heart and
lungs, or I reverse its evolution and imagine it as a lizard. I
see its scaled legs and that naked ring around a shiny eye;
I shrink and deplume its feathers to lizard scales, unhorn

its lipless mouth, and set it stalking dragonflies, cool-eyed, under a palmetto. Then I reverse the process once again, quickly; its forelegs unfurl, its scales hatch feathers and soften. It takes to the air seeking cool forests; it sings songs. This is what I have on my chimney; it might as well keep me awake out of wonder as rage.

Some reputable scientists, even today, are not wholly satisfied with the notion that the song of birds is strictly and solely a territorial claim. It's an important point. We've been on earth all these years and we still don't know for certain why birds sing. We need someone to unlock the code to this foreign language and give us the key; we need a new Rosetta stone. Or should we learn, as I had to, each new word one by one? It could be that a bird sings I am sparrow, sparrow, sparrow, as Gerard Manley Hopkins suggests: "myself it speaks and spells, Crying *What I do is me: for that I came.*" Sometimes birdsong seems just like the garbled speech of infants. There is a certain age at which a child looks at you in all earnestness and delivers a long, pleased speech in all the true inflections of spoken English, but with not one recognizable syllable. There is no way you can tell the child that if language had been a melody, he had mastered it and done well, but that since it was in fact a sense, he had botched it utterly.

Today I watched and heard a wren, a sparrow, and the mockingbird singing. My brain started to trill why why why, what is the meaning meaning meaning? It's not that they know something we don't; we know much more than they do, and surely they don't even know why they sing. No; we have been as usual asking the wrong question. It does not matter a hoot what the mockingbird on the chimney is singing. If the mockingbird were chirping to give us the long-sought formulae for a unified field theory, the point would be only slightly less irrelevant. The real and proper question is: Why is it beautiful? I hesitate to use the word so baldly, but the question is there. The question is there since I take it as given, as I have said, that beauty is something objectively performed—the tree that falls in the forest—having being externally, stumbled across or missed, as real and present as both sides of the moon. This modified lizard's song welling out of the fireplace has a wild, utterly foreign music; it becomes more and more beautiful as it becomes more and more familiar. If the lyric is simply "mine mine mine," then why the extravagance of the score? It has the liquid, intricate sound of every creek's tumble over every configuration of rock creek-bottom in the country. Who, telegraphing a message, would trouble to transmit a five-act play, or Coleridge's "Kubla Khan," and who, receiving the message, could understand it? Beauty itself is the language to which we have no key; it is the mute cipher, the cryptogram, the uncracked, unbroken code. And it could be that for beauty, as it turned out to be for French, that there is no key, that "oui" will never make sense in our language but only in its own, and that we need to start all over again, on a new continent, learning the strange syllables one by one.

FROM *Pilgrim at Tinker Creek*

A Raven's Call

BERND HEINRICH

The author of this remarkable study of the behavior of ravens, one that impelled him to rise in the morning before the ravens in order to observe them at their feeding rituals, teaches biology at the University of Vermont. In these paragraphs, he speculates about what may lie behind a raven's call.

Birds are primarily emotional beings, and their responses to emotional drives are probably much more direct than ours are, since human reactions are tempered by reason. Emotions are more "primitive" than reason, and I presume that many animals have very similar emotions to ours but, since they are driven by emotions, to a stronger degree. One major expression of emotions is vocalization, but there is no *a priori* reason to suppose that when a raven feels sad, it makes a sound that sounds "sad" to our ears. It could just as well sound "happy."

Many animals make arbitrary sounds that, like codes, have specific meaning. Thus, the mating calls of different grasshoppers, cicadas, or birds are very distinct, and to our ears they have no emotional content. Similarly, other calls of a sparrow, dove, or warbler also have little meaning to us except through the intellect when we figure them out. It surprises me, therefore, that many of the raven's calls sometimes display emotions that I, as a mammal for whom they are not intended, can feel.

When a raven pair is intimate with each other, they make cooing noises that *sound* soft and tender. When a situation arises where I expect a raven to be angry, it gives deep rasping calls that convey anger to my ears. I also feel I can detect a raven's surprise, happiness, bravado, and self-aggrandizement from its voice and body language. I cannot identify such a range of emotions in a sparrow or in a hawk.

Both Konrad Lorenz and Tony Angell describe the invitation to join in flight given by their pet ravens Roah and Macaw, respectively. According to Lorenz, to invite a family member to follow, each raven flew close over its keeper from the back at good speed, and in passing it wobbled with its tail and called a sonorous yet sharply metallic "krackrack-rack." (Roah also tried to lure Lorenz away from places the bird avoided, but instead of the rack-rack-rack calls, it mimicked its own name!) Nothing is known about the context of this behavior in wild ravens. However, Nelson quotes Koyukon native hunters: "If a raven sees people hunting, it will occasionally help them find game. It flies ahead, then toward an animal that is visible from above, calling *ggaagga—ggaagga* (animal—animal). He does that so he'll get his share from what the hunter leaves behind."

And "hunters also see a raven tuck its wing and roll over in the sky to show where bear or moose is standing." Is this folkore or fact? A trapper/hunter from Nenana, Alaska, with whom I talked at length about ravens volunteered that he had seen the display. (I had not mentioned it to him.) He told me that a raven, after dipping right and left, fanning its tail, dived over a place in the woods while making a specific call. After the raven repeated the maneuver, the man had "the distinct impression the raven was trying to show me something." He followed and discovered a moose! Coincidence? Do ravens guide wolves and other "dangerous" animals to hunt for them? It is possible, but I am personally skeptical. I later suspected this trapper had read Lorenz more closely than Nature, and when I asked him months later, in a different context, I found out: "Yes, I have read *all* of Lorenz!" I dearly wished that he had not; as a scientist, I cannot trust complex observations that are fitted into a preexisting mold of the mind. The weight of consistently repeatable observations themselves have to create the mold or the idea.

FROM *Ravens in Winter*

Bird Song Compared to Human Music

CHARLES HARTSHORNE

They [birds] are the true masters.
DVOŘÁK

Charles Hartshorne taught philosophy at the University of Texas. He was also a field associate of the Laboratory of Ornithology at Cornell and a longtime student of animal behavior.

A great naturalist once guided me to a spot where we could hear a pair of Black-throated Wrens (*Thryothorus atrogularis*) of restricted geographical range whose lovely song duet few seem to have commented upon. As we left the spot, having heard two neighboring pairs sing animated musical duets, he addressed the birds, saying, "Thank you for the concert." Then he muttered, "Those who say bird

song is not music are fools of the first water." A fairer judg-
ment might be that such persons are either not well acquainted with bird songs or have not learned to distinguish
between objective and subjective factors in aesthetic matters
or between primitive, largely instinctive, and sophisticated
forms of music.

Music, objectively regarded, is to be characterized in two
ways, according as we take into account only the patterns
of sound that are produced or also the behavior-setting of
this production. Let us first consider the sounds alone, and
taken singly. Birds utter both "noises" and musical "tones,"
and it is the latter which are more conspicuous in their
songs, especially the more "melodious" songs. The tones can
be as pure as in human music, though often they are between noises and tones. There are flute-like, truly chime- or
bell-like, violin- or guitar-like, even organ-like, tones to be
heard from birds. Some are almost as tender as a boy so-
prano, e.g., those of nightingale-thrushes (*Catharus* spp.) or
the Olive Whistler of southern Queensland.

It may be that statistically birds use noises more and tones
less in their singing than man does. Another relative difference is that avian singers, being mostly rather small,
favor high pitches, which often sound thin and rather un-
satisfying to man. However, there is some evidence that
small Songbirds, singing in this way, have slightly higher
upper limits of hearing, so that what to us are shrill sounds
may be more "mellow" to the birds. This is supported by
the fact that in general birds sing mostly near the middle of
their pitch ranges, the lower limits of which are often much
higher than in man.

Birds tend to use very brief sounds and may crowd several times as many distinct notes into a second of singing as
a human singer can. Here, too, the biological significance

of the difference is uncertain, since we have every reason to think that birds live at a faster tempo altogether than man does, and have a far higher, perhaps ten times as high or even higher, temporal resolving power for sounds. Thus what are excessively brief and hence insignificant elements of auditory experience for us need not be so for birds. The markedly higher temperatures, the faster heartbeat and other reactions, and perhaps the shorter and simpler neural paths point to the same conclusion. Thus in both pitch and tempo, especially the latter, we are more likely to under- than overestimate avian music.

In both respects also there are numerous exceptions to the stated differences between birds and man. I cannot think of any human music with a slower pace than that of the Varied Thrust (*Zoothera naevius*) of the Pacific coast of North America. One race (or species?) of the Nightingale Wren (*Microcerculus marginatus*) sings one note every 3–4 or more seconds. And as to pitch, many birds, for example, the Bifasciated Lark, have what is for us a comfortable pitch range.

Another only partly true statement about avian song is that bird notes tend to be slurred (as shown by slanting lines in audiospectrograms), sliding continuously up or down. However, many are not slurred appreciably. In one case scientists showed that an apparent slur in the singing of the Townsend's Solitaire (*Myadestes townsendi*) is really a "glissando," a descending series of very brief notes. With birds' faster tempo this may often be true. But some bird notes seem well sustained on one pitch, e.g., the opening notes (½ second) of most Hermit Thrush patterns and most notes in the singing of the Andean Solitaire (*Myadestes ralloides*) and of the Desert or Bifasciated Lark. The Pileated Tinamou (*Crypturellus soui*) has some unslurred notes a second and a half in duration. Some human music, especially in Turkey and the Near East generally, favors slurs and quavers.

It is suspected that birds react somewhat to features of sound waves (besides those of frequency and amplitude) to which human response is limited. However, this difference between us and birds cannot be very great, because, for physical reasons, sensitivity to the aspects of sound waves which we cannot experience conflicts in principle with sensitivity to small pitch differences, and we know that birds discriminate pitches very well. Here, too, we are not hopelessly ill equipped to appreciate bird song.

Now we turn to the order or pattern of the sounds. "Order is the vast realm lying between the deadly extremes of chaos and mechanization." This dictum of a great musicologist applies to bird song. Very few songs even tempt one to think of them as mere random handfuls of notes, and equally few seem wholly mechanical in their regularity.

FROM *Born to Sing*

Part Three

Art and Ritual

The fact that birds have feathers makes them masters of the air. In addition, they can coexist with almost all of the earth's environments. Each species mirrors the individual nature of its chosen habitat, from the little brown wren that is part of the forest floor, to the water ouzel which is inseparable from the streams and waterfalls it inhabits. The birds can be as extravagant as a bird of paradise in New Guinea, or as appropriate as a chickadee to a gray, New England tree. The bird is an exterior representation of any given landscape; its motions and ritualized behavior follow rhythmic cycles. The insights we gain from watching and listening to them are potentially inexhaustible. They amount to an exploration of spaces that lie hidden in ourselves.

The Frigate Pelican

MARIANNE MOORE

Anyone who has ever seen a pelican or a frigatebird might be puzzled by the title of this poem. It obviously describes the flight of that black pirate of a bird, with its rakish wings, once called the man o'war bird and now the magnificent frigatebird, Frigata magnificens, *which bears little resemblance to a pelican. The answer lies in Marianne Moore's notes to the poem, which give credit for the name "frigate pelican" to Audubon.*

↣

Rapidly cruising or lying on the air there is a bird
   that realizes Rasselas's friend's project
  of wings uniting levity with strength. This
     hell-diver, frigate bird, hurricane-
bird; unless swift is the proper word
    for him, the storm omen when

he flies close to the waves, should be seen
   fishing, although oftener
   he appears to prefer

to take, on the wing, from industrious crude-winged
      species,
   the fish they have caught, and is seldom successless.
   A marvel of grace, no matter how fast his
      victim may fly or how often may
turn. The others with similar ease,
   slowly rising once more,
      move out to the top
      of the circle and stop

and blow back, allowing the wind to reverse their
      direction—
   unlike the more stalwart swan that can ferry the
   woodcutter's two children home. Make hay; keep
      the shop; I have one sheep; were a less
limber animal's mottoes. This one
   finds sticks for the swan's-down dress
of his child to rest upon and would
      not know Gretel from Hänsel.
      As impassioned Handel

meant for a lawyer and a masculine German domestic
   career—clandestinely studied the harpsichord
   and never was known to have fallen in love,
      the unconfiding frigate bird hides
      in the height and in the majestic
         display of his art. He glides
      a hundred feet or quivers about
         as charred paper behaves—full
         of feints; and an eagle

of vigilance. . . . *Festina lente.* Be gay
    civilly? How so? "If I do well I am blessed
    whether any bless me or not, and if I do
        ill I am cursed." We watch the moon rise
on the Susquehanna. In his way,
        this most romantic bird flies
to a more mundane place, the mangrove
    swamp to sleep. He wastes the moon.
    But he, and others, soon

rise from the bough and though flying, are able to foil the
    tired
    moment of danger that lays on heart and lungs the
    weight of the python that crushes to powder.

FROM *Complete Poems of Marianne Moore*

Evolution and the Bird of Paradise

EDWARD O. WILSON

The following is taken from Biophilia, *by the renowned socio-biologist and professor of entomology at Harvard, E. O. Wilson. One of his many accomplishments has been to co-author, with Bert Hölldobler, an exhaustive study of ants, a lifetime preoccupation. Wilson has inspired a generation of students, as well as countless readers, to see animal communities as highly social and cooperative. They are not to be reduced in our estimation to an inferior status. Both ants and humans are a functional part of the greater organization born of the ancestry of the planet.*

⁂

The jewel of the setting is the male Emperor of Germany bird of paradise (*Paradisaea guilielmi*), arguably the most beautiful bird in the world, certainly one of the twenty or so most striking in appearance. By moving quietly along secondary trails you might glimpse one on a lichen-encrusted branch near the tree tops. Its head is shaped like that of a crow—no surprise because the birds of paradise and crows have a close common lineage—but there the outward resemblance to any ordinary bird ends. The crown and upper breast of the bird are metallic oil-green and shine in the sunlight. The back is glossy yellow, the wings and tail deep reddish maroon. Tufts of ivory-white plumes sprout from the flanks and sides of the breast, turning lacy in texture toward the tips. The plume rectrices continue on as wirelike appendages past the breast and tail for a distance equal to the full length of the bird. The bill is blue-gray, the eyes clear amber, the claws brown and black.

In the mating season the male joins others in leks, common courtship arenas in the upper tree branches, where they display their dazzling ornaments to the more somberly caparisoned females. The male spreads his wings and vibrates them while lifting the gossamer flank plumes. He calls loudly with bubbling and flutelike notes and turns upside down on the perch, spreading the wings and tail and pointing his rectrices skyward. The dance then reaches a climax as he fluffs up the green breast feathers and opens out the flank plumes until they form a brilliant white circle around his body, with only the head, tail, and wings projecting beyond. The male sways gently from side to side, causing the plumes to wave gracefully as if caught in an errant breeze. Seen from a distance his body now resembles a spinning and slightly out-of-focus white disk.

This improbable spectacle in the Huon forest has been fashioned by millions of generations of natural selection in which males competed and females made choices, and the accouterments of display were driven to a visual extreme. But this is only one trait, seen in physiological time and thought about at a single level of causation. Beneath its plumed surface, the Emperor of Germany bird of paradise possesses an architecture culminating an ancient history, with details exceeding those that can be imagined from the naturalist's simple daylight record of color and dance.

Consider one such bird for a moment in the analytic manner, as an object of biological research. Encoded within its chromosomes is the developmental program that led with finality to a male *Paradisaea guilielmi*. The completed nervous system is a structure of fiber tracts more complicated than any existing computer, and as challenging as all the rain forests of New Guinea surveyed on foot. A microscopic study will someday permit us to trace the events that culminate in the electric commands carried by the efferent neurons to the skeletal-muscular system and reproduce, in part, the dance of the courting male. This machinery can be dissected and understood by proceeding to the level of the cell, to enzymatic catalysis, microfilament configuration, and active sodium transport during electric discharge. Because biology sweeps the full range of space and time, there will be more discoveries renewing the sense of wonder at each step of research. By altering the scale of perception to the micrometer and millisecond, the laboratory scientist parallels the trek of the naturalist across the land. He looks out from his own version of the mountain crest. His spirit of adventure, as well as personal history of hardship, misdirection, and triumph, are fundamentally the same.

Described this way, the bird of paradise may seem to have been turned into a metaphor of what humanists dislike most about science: that it reduces nature and is insensitive to art, that scientists are conquistadors who melt down the Inca gold. But bear with me a minute. Science is not just analytic; it is also synthetic. It uses artlike intuition and imagery. In the early stages, individual behavior can be analyzed to the level of genes and neurosensory cells, whereupon the phenomena have indeed been mechanically reduced. In the synthetic phase, though, even the most elementary activity of these biological units creates rich and subtle patterns at the levels of organism and society. The outer qualities of *Paradisaea guilielmi,* its plumes, dance, and daily life, are functional traits open to a deeper understanding through the exact description of their constituent parts. They can be redefined as holistic properties that alter our perception and emotion in surprising and pleasant ways.

There will come a time when the bird of paradise is reconstituted by the synthesis of all the hard-won analytic information. The mind, bearing a newfound power, will journey back to the familiar world of seconds and centimeters. Once again the glittering plumage takes form and is viewed at a distance through a network of leaves and mist. Then we see the bright eye open, the head swivel, the wings extend. But the familiar motions are viewed across a far greater range of cause and effect. The species is understood more completely; misleading illusions have given way to light and wisdom of a greater degree. One turn of the cycle of intellect is then complete. The excitement of the scientist's search for the true material nature of the species recedes, to be replaced in part by the more enduring responses of the hunter and poet.

What are these ancient responses? The full answer can only be given through a combined idiom of science and the humanities, whereby the investigation turns back into itself. The human being, like the bird of paradise, awaits our examination in the analytic-synthetic manner. As always by honored tradition, feeling and myth can be viewed at a distance through physiological time, idiosyncratically, in the manner of traditional art. But they can also be penetrated more deeply than ever was possible in the prescientific age, to their physical basis in the processes of mental development, the brain structure, and indeed the genes themselves. It may even be possible to trace them back through time past cultural history to the evolutionary origins of human nature. With each new phase of synthesis to emerge from biological inquiry, the humanities will expand their reach and capability. In symmetric fashion, with each redirection of the humanities, science will add dimensions to human biology.

FROM *Biophilia*

The Water Ouzel

*In this graphic description of the water ouzel, or dipper, bird
and habitat find a perfect match. "The ouzel of all birds dares
to enter a white torrent." Behind the torrent is a little nest made
of green moss; in the nest, the eggs like bubbles of foam are laid,
just out of reach. This outwardly dangerous affinity is actually
the bird's assurance of lasting life, its form and spirit. It practices
water magic to the end of time.*

❧

The waterfalls of the Sierra are frequented by only one
bird—the ouzel or water thrush (*Cinclus Mexicanus,* Sw.).
He is a singularly joyous and lovable little fellow, about the
size of a robin, clad in a plain waterproof suit of bluish gray,
with a tinge of chocolate on the head and shoulders. In
form he is about as smoothly plump and compact as a peb-

ble that had been whirled in a pot-hole, the flowing contour of his body being interrupted only by his strong feet and bill, the crisp wing-tips, and the upslanted wren-like tail.

Among all the countless waterfalls I have met in the course of ten years' exploration in the Sierra, whether among the icy peaks, or warm foot-hills, or in the profound yosemitic cañons of the middle region, not one was found without its ouzel. No cañon is too cold for this little bird, none too lonely, provided it be rich in falling water. Find a fall, or cascade, or rushing rapid, anywhere upon a clear stream, and there you will surely find its complementary ouzel, flitting about in the spray, diving in foaming eddies, whirling like a leaf among beaten foam-bells; ever vigorous and enthusiastic, yet self-contained, and neither seeking nor shunning your company.

If disturbed while dipping about in the margin shallows, he either sets off with a rapid whir to some other feeding-ground up or down the stream, or alights on some half-submerged rock or snag out in the current, and immediately begins to nod and curtsey like a wren, turning his head from side to side with many other odd dainty movements that never fail to fix the attention of the observer.

He is the mountain streams' own darling, the humming-bird of blooming waters, loving rocky ripple slopes and sheets of foam as a bee loves flowers, as a lark loves sunshine and meadows. Among all the mountain birds, none has cheered me so much in my lonely wanderings—none so unfailingly. For both in winter and summer he sings, sweetly, cheerily, independent alike of sunshine and of love, requiring no other inspiration than the stream on which he dwells. While water sings, so must he, in heat or cold, calm or storm, ever attuning his voice in sure accord; low in the drought of summer and the drought of winter, but never silent.

During the golden days of Indian summer, after most of the snow has been melted, and the mountain streams have become feeble—a succession of silent pools, linked together by shallow, transparent currents and strips of silvery lace-work—then the song of the ouzel is at its lowest ebb. But as soon as the winter clouds have bloomed, and the mountain treasuries are once more replenished with snow, the voices of the streams and ouzels increase in strength and richness until the flood season of early summer. Then the torrents chant their noblest anthems, and then is the flood-time of our songster's melody. As for weather, dark days and sun days are the same to him. The voices of most song-birds, however joyous, suffer a long winter eclipse; but the ouzel sings on through all the seasons and every kind of storm. Indeed, no storm can be more violent than those of the waterfalls in the midst of which he delights to dwell. However dark and boisterous the weather, snowing, blow-ing, or cloudy, all the same he sings, and with never a note of sadness. No need of spring sunshine to thaw *his* song, for it never freezes. Never shall you hear anything wintery from *his* warm breast; no pinched cheeping, no wavering notes between sorrow and joy; his mellow, fluty voice is ever tuned to downright gladness, as free from dejection as cock-crowing.

It is pitiful to see wee frost-pinched sparrows on cold mornings in the mountain groves shaking the snow from their feathers, and hopping about as if anxious to be cheery, then hastening back to their hidings out of the wind, puff-ing out their breast feathers over their toes, and subsiding among the leaves, cold and breakfastless, while the snow continues to fall, and there is no sign of clearing. But the ouzel never calls forth a single touch of pity; not because he is strong to endure, but rather because he seems to live a charmed life beyond the reach of every influence that makes endurance necessary. . . .

What may be regarded as the separate songs of the ouzel are exceedingly difficult of description, because they are so variable and at the same time so confluent. Though I have been acquainted with my favorite ten years, and during most of this time have heard him sing nearly every day, I still detect notes and strains that seem new to me. Nearly all of his music is sweet and tender, lapsing from his round breast like water over the smooth lip of a pool, then breaking farther on into a sparkling foam of melodious notes, which glow with subdued enthusiasm, yet without expressing much of the strong, gushing ecstasy of the bobolink or skylark.

The more striking strains are perfect arabesques of melody, composed of a few full, round, mellow notes, embroidered with delicate trills which fade and melt in long slender cadences. In a general way his music is that of the streams refined and spiritualized. The deep booming notes of the falls are in it, the trills of rapids, the gurgling of margin eddies, the low whispering of level reaches, and the sweet tinkle of separate drops oozing from the end of mosses and falling into tranquil pools.

The ouzel never sings in chorus with other birds, nor with his kind, but only with the streams. And like flowers that bloom beneath the surface of the ground, some of our favorite's best song-blossoms never rise above the surface of the heavier music of the water. I have often observed him singing in the midst of beaten spray, his music completely buried beneath the water's roar; yet I knew he was surely singing by his gestures and the movements of his bill.

His food, as far as I have noticed, consists of all kinds of water insects, which in summer are chiefly procured along shallow margins. Here he wades about ducking his head under water and deftly turning over pebbles and fallen leaves with his bill, seldom choosing to go into deep water where he has to use his wings in diving.

He seems to be especially fond of the larvæ of mosquitoes, found in abundance attached to the bottom of smooth rock channels where the current is shallow. When feeding in such places he wades upstream, and often while his head is under water the swift current is deflected upward along the glossy curves of his neck and shoulders, in the form of a clear, crystalline shell, which fairly incloses him like a bell-glass, the shell being broken and re-formed as he lifts and dips his head; while ever and anon he sidles out to where the too powerful current carries him off his feet; then he dexterously rises on the wing and goes gleaning again in shallower places.

But during the winter, when the stream banks are embossed in snow, and the streams themselves are chilled nearly to the freezing-point, so that the snow falling into them in stormy weather is not wholly dissolved, but forms a thin, blue sludge, thus rendering the current opaque—then he seeks the deeper portions of the main rivers, where he may dive to clear water beneath the sludge. Or he repairs to some open lake or millpond, at the bottom of which he feeds in safety. . . .

The ouzel seldom swims more than a few yards on the surface, for, not being web-footed, he makes rather slow progress, but by means of his strong, crisp wings he swims,

or rather flies, with celerity under the surface, often to considerable distances. But it is in withstanding the force of
heavy rapids that his strength of wing in this respect is most
strikingly manifested. The following may be regarded as a
fair illustration of his power of sub-aquatic flight. One
stormy morning in winter when the Merced River was blue
and green with unmelted snow, I observed one of my ouzels
perched on a snag out in the midst of a swift-rushing rapid,
singing cheerily, as if everything was just to his mind; and
while I stood on the bank admiring him, he suddenly
plunged into the sludgy current, leaving his song abruptly
broken off. After feeding a minute or two at the bottom,
and when one would suppose that he must inevitably be
swept far downstream, he emerged just where he went
down, alighted on the same snag, showered the water beads
from his feathers, and continued his unfinished song, seemingly in tranquil ease as if it had suffered no interruption.

The ouzel alone of all birds dares to enter a white torrent. And though strictly terrestrial in structure, no other is
so inseparably related to water, not even the duck, or the
bold ocean albatross, or the stormy petrel. For ducks go
ashore as soon as they finish feeding in undisturbed places,
and very often make long flights overland from lake to lake
or field to field. The same is true of most other aquatic
birds. But the ouzel, born on the brink of a stream, or on
a snag or boulder in the midst of it, seldom leaves it for a
single moment. For, notwithstanding he is often on the
wing, he never flies overland, but whirs with rapid, quail-
like beat above the stream, tracing all its windings. Even
when the stream is quite small, say from five to ten feet
wide, he seldom shortens his flight by crossing a bend, however abrupt it may be; and even when disturbed by meeting
some one on the bank, he prefers to fly over one's head, to

dodging out over the ground. When, therefore, his flight along a crooked stream is viewed endwise, it appears most strikingly wavered—a description on the air of every curve with lightning-like rapidity.

The vertical curves and angles of the most precipitous torrents he traces with the same rigid fidelity, swooping down the inclines of cascades, dropping sheer over dizzy falls amid the spray, and ascending with the same fearlessness and ease, seldom seeking to lessen the steepness of the acclivity by beginning to ascend before reaching the base of the fall. No matter though it may be several hundred feet in height he holds straight on, as if about to dash headlong into the throng of booming rockets, then darts abruptly upward, and, after alighting at the top of the precipice to rest a moment, proceeds to feed and sing. His flight is solid and impetuous, without any intermission of wing-beats—one homogeneous buzz like that of a laden bee on its way home. And while thus buzzing freely from fall to fall, he is frequently heard giving utterance to a long outdrawn train of unmodulated notes, in no way connected with his song, but corresponding closely with his flight in sustained vigor.

Were the flights of all the ouzels in the Sierra traced on a chart, they would indicate the direction of the flow of the entire system of ancient glaciers, from about the period of the breaking up of the ice-sheet until near the close of the glacial winter; because the streams which the ouzels so rigidly follow are, with the unimportant exceptions of a few side tributaries, all flowing in channels eroded for them out of the solid flank of the range by the vanished glaciers—the streams tracing the ancient glaciers, the ouzels tracing the streams. Nor do we find so complete compliance to glacial conditions in the life of any other mountain bird, or animal of any kind. Bears frequently accept the pathways laid down by glaciers as the easiest to travel; but they often leave them and cross over from cañon to cañon. So also, most of the birds trace the moraines to some extent, because the forests are growing on them. But they wander far, crossing the cañons from grove to grove, and draw exceedingly angular and complicated courses.

The ouzel's nest is one of the most extraordinary pieces of bird architecture I ever saw, odd and novel in design, perfectly fresh and beautiful, and in every way worthy of the genius of the little builder. It is about a foot in diameter, round and bossy in outline, with a neatly arched opening near the bottom, somewhat like an old-fashioned brick oven, or Hottentot's hut. It is built almost exclusively of green and yellow mosses, chiefly the beautiful fronded hypnum that covers the rocks and old drift-logs in the vicinity of waterfalls. These are deftly interwoven, and felted together into a charming little hut; and so situated that many of the outer mosses continue to flourish as if they had not been plucked. A few fine, silky-stemmed grasses are occasionally found interwoven with the mosses, but, with the exception of a thin layer lining the floor, their presence seems accidental, as they are of a species found growing with the mosses and are probably plucked with them. The site chosen for this curious mansion is usually some little rock shelf within reach of the lighter particles of the spray of a waterfall, so that its walls are kept green and growing, at least during the time of high water.

No harsh lines are presented by any portion of the nest as seen in place, but when removed from its shelf, the back and bottom, and sometimes a portion of the top, is found quite sharply angular, because it is made to conform to the surface of the rock upon which and against which it is built, the little architect always taking advantage of slight crevices and protuberances that may chance to offer, to render his structure stable by means of a kind of gripping and dovetailing.

In choosing a building-spot, concealment does not seem to be taken into consideration; yet notwithstanding the nest is large and guilelessly exposed to view, it is far from being easily detected, chiefly because it swells forward like any other bulging moss cushion growing naturally in such situations. This is more especially the case where the nest is kept fresh by being well sprinkled. Sometimes these romantic little huts have their beauty enhanced by rock ferns and grasses that spring up around the mossy walls, or in front of the doorsill, dripping with crystal beads.

Furthermore, at certain hours of the day, when the sunshine is poured down at the required angle, the whole mass of the spray enveloping the fairy establishment is brilliantly irised; and it is through so glorious a rainbow atmosphere as this that some of our blessed ouzels obtain their first peep at the world. . . .

In these moss huts three or four eggs are laid, white like foam bubbles; and well may the little birds hatched from them sing water-songs, for they hear them all their lives, and even before they are born.

I have often observed the young just out of the nest making their odd gestures, and seeming in every way as much at home as their experienced parents, like young bees on their first excursions to the flower fields. No amount of familiarity with people and their ways seems to change them in the least. To all appearance their behavior is just the same on seeing a man for the first time, as when they have seen him frequently. . . .

Love for songbirds, with their sweet human voices, appears to be more common and unfailing than love for flowers. Every one loves flowers to some extent, at least in life's fresh morning, attracted by them as instinctively as hummingbirds and bees. Even the young Digger Indians have sufficient love for the brightest of those found growing on the mountains to gather them and braid them as decorations for the hair. And I was glad to discover, through the few Indians that could be induced to talk on the subject, that they have names for the wild rose and the lily, and other conspicuous flowers, whether available as food or otherwise. Most men, however, whether savage or civilized, become apathetic toward all plants that have no other apparent use than the use of beauty. But fortunately one's first instinctive love of songbirds is never wholly obliterated, no matter what the influences upon our lives may be. I have often been delighted to see a pure, spiritual glow come into the countenances of hard business men and old miners, when a songbird chanced to alight near them. Nevertheless, the little mouthful of meat that swells out the breasts of some songbirds is too often the cause of their death. Larks and robins in particular are brought to market in hundreds. But fortunately the ouzel has no enemy so eager to eat his little body as to follow him into the mountain solitudes. I never knew him to be chased even by hawks.

An acquaintance of mine, a sort of foot-hill mountaineer, had a pet cat, a great, dozy, overgrown creature, about as broad-shouldered as a lynx. During the winter, while the snow lay deep, the mountaineer sat in his lonely cabin among the Pines smoking his pipe and wearing the dull time away. Tom was his sole companion, sharing his bed, and sitting beside him on a stool with much the same drowsy expression of eye as his master. The goodnatured bachelor was content with his hard fare of soda bread and bacon, but Tom, the only creature in the world acknowledging dependence on him, must needs be provided with fresh meat. Accordingly he bestirred himself to contrive squirrel traps, and waded the snowy woods with his gun, making sad havoc among the few winter birds, sparing neither robin, sparrow, nor tiny nuthatch, and the pleasure of seeing Tom eat and grow fat was his great reward.

One cold afternoon, while hunting along the river-bank, he noticed a plain-feathered little bird skipping about in the shallows, and immediately raised his gun. But just then the confiding songster began to sing, and after listening to his summery melody the charmed hunter turned away, saying, "Bless your little heart, I can't shoot you, not even for Tom."

Even so far north as icy Alaska, I have found my glad singer. When I was exploring the glaciers between Mount Fairweather and the Stickeen River, one cold day in November, after trying in vain to force a way through the innumerable icebergs of Sum Dum Bay to the great glaciers at the head of it, I was weary and baffled and sat resting in my canoe convinced at last that I would have to leave this part of my work for another year. Then I began to plan my escape to open water before the young ice which was beginning to form should shut me in. While I thus lingered drifting with the bergs, in the midst of these gloomy forebodings and all the terrible glacial desolation and grandeur, I suddenly heard the well-known whir of an ouzel's wings, and, looking up saw my little comforter coming straight across the ice from the shore. In a second or two he was with me, flying three times round my head with a happy salute, as if saying, "Cheer up, old friend; you see I'm here, and all's well." Then he flew back to the shore, alighted on the topmost jag of a stranded iceberg, and began to nod and bow as though he were on one of his favorite boulders in the midst of a sunny Sierra cascade.

The species is distributed all along the mountain ranges of the Pacific Coast from Alaska to Mexico, and east to the Rocky Mountains. Nevertheless, it is as yet comparatively little known. Audubon and Wilson did not meet it. Swainson was, I believe, the first naturalist to describe a specimen from Mexico. Specimens were shortly afterward procured by Drummond near the sources of the Athabasca River, between the fifty-fourth and fifty-sixth parallels; and it has been collected by nearly all of the numerous exploring expeditions undertaken of late through our Western States and Territories; for it never fails to engage the attention of naturalists in a very particular manner.

Such then, is our little cinclus, beloved of every one who is so fortunate as to know him. Tracing on strong wing every curve of the most precipitous torrents from one extremity of the Sierra to the other; not fearing to follow them through their darkest gorges and coldest snow-tunnels; acquainted with every waterfall, echoing their divine music; and throughout the whole of their beautiful lives interpreting all that we in our unbelief call terrible in the utterances of torrents and storms, as only varied expressions of God's eternal love.

FROM *The Wilderness World of John Muir*

Ritual in Terns

JOHN HAY

An incident centering on spring courtship between a pair of Roseate terns on the tidal flats off Cape Cod Bay suggests a parallel equation with the human spirit. (Fishing people all over the world are now experiencing a precipitous decline of a food which was once a vital and even sacred part of community life.)

⟫

Vision, in its less material sense, is in the mind's eye, seen in a dream, or in a trance. The original native people of America followed the wilderness from which all fundamental dreams must come, and found "spirit helpers" who would guide them for the rest of their lives. Through "vision quests" individuals worshipped the Eagle—the Thunderbird—or the Morning Star. A Plains Indian told the anthropologist Robert Lowie that he had a feather which he kept as a remembrance of his vision of a bird, and that it was the greatest treasure in the world. Behind the tangible lies the revelation of the spirit.

One might argue that vision in our violent, contemporary world embraces disconnected dreams and public hallucinations, since we have been disengaged from an intangible entity we call "the environment." The animals, on the other hand, not knowing any alternative, as we might put it, but simply knowing, keep the earth in being. Out of endless periods of trial and error, the terns know their direction and where they are, through exceptional abilities of sight and inner timing, moving as the earth moves. We do not apply vision in this sense to a bird. We assume that sight is a mechanical feature that describes adaptation and closeness to habitat, but below that spirit cannot be called upon in any useful way. This implies that it is we who do not know, and may have lost our way. As the terns are true fishermen, we can at least call on them to tell us where the food of the spirit can be found.

Animals, to our way of thinking, do not behave religiously, though we can hardly refuse them their role in ceremony. Surely the ritualistic behavior of the terns obeys the outward signs of an inner grace, which cannot be monopolized by the human race. Why should fish, so central to their existence, not be sacred to the terns? At the very least, they are actors on behalf of what can never be transgressed.

In the morning, the braided sands lead off at low tide under a light fog, through which the sunlight has started to burn. The south wind cuffs away at sheets of shallow water, making feather patterns of purple and gray. A pair of Roseates are out on the tidal flats, acting out the primal style. Seen from behind, the female, head and neck proudly stretched, has her wings parted like a bow that reminds me of the shape of a horseshoe crab, or of a flounder. The male, partly bent, holds a fish, a glint of silver in the drifting fog.

A fish, of the great race of fishes, with the color of reflecting waters. They are a sunset-yellow; coppery; pink and red; a steely blue; intensely silver like a herring, or a smelt; blue-black, green and tawny yellow like a mackerel. There is no end to the changing reflections of light and water, as witnessed in their scales. In courtship, a fish becomes more than a food: it is a symbol, the ritualized body of the world.

It is a strange thing, when you first become aware of it, to see in these birds the transmutation of substance into the realm of the spirit, but "stereotyped ritual" is hardly enough. One day, watching this performance, I thought to myself: "Why, of course! 'This is my body.' "

Food has always been central to religious rites. And the human ceremonials that join a family through food and wine, or wife to husband, are not alien to a tern's offering of a fish to its prospective mate.

The fish, so profoundly a part of the tern's life and livelihood, and with which it must feel some irreplaceable attachment, is also a mark of what must live forever. As a ceremonial object, it indicates that what it symbolizes cannot be utterly consumed. In all this basic ritualizing might be the seeds of the human concept of immortality.

The fish itself is a mystery, as well as a known reality. The first spring alewives migrating into fresh water, flashing through the rocks of a down-falling stream, are silver spear-heads thrown in by the energy of an unknown sea. I who am also of the living store of earth, meet them symbolically. I now see fish in the way I first did, before a later age when I might imagine that experience had taught me better. So the terns themselves seem all youth and no old age.

FROM *The Bird of Light*

The Dance of the Whooping Crane

ROBERT PORTER ALLEN

*This splendid bird, almost eradicated from the American con-
tinent but kept from extinction through careful management,
has become a symbol of a once-thriving wilderness. The whooping crane population may never have exceeded several thousand
even before the white man came. Nevertheless, John James Audubon described their southerly, fall migration as comprising
flocks of twenty or thirty birds spreading from Illinois into Kentucky until they reached the Carolinas, Florida, and "countries
bordering on Mexico," where they spent the winter.*

*Today the population of whooping cranes has risen from only
15 in 1941 to about one hundred and fifty. After wintering in
Aransas, one of the few undisturbed areas left which these very
shy birds can tolerate, they fly twenty-five hundred miles north*

on their spring migration to Wood Buffalo National Park, in Canada's Northwest Territories. The following account of their displays on their last remaining refuge at Port Aransas, Texas, is by Robert Porter Allen.

The dances begin in mid-December or a little thereafter. These spectacular performances mark the beginning of a new breeding cycle. With the immense size of the birds, this dance is one of the great dramas of the bird world. It may begin quite suddenly, as the family group is standing idly on a ridge of salt-flat grass, preening their feathers. The male bird turns, walks off into the shallow water, and stretches, raising his wings over his back, bending forward slightly as he does so. All at once he starts to dance, bowing toward the female, who now steps into the water beside him. Raising his satin-white wings with their jet-black tips to the fullest extent, he leaps high in the air, executing a half turn before landing. The female is now in the formalized attitude of a dancing crane, her neck arched, wings and plumes slightly raised, whole body stiff and yet graceful, like that of a ballerina. They begin by leaping together, but it is the male who leaps most often, in what appears to be a perfect frenzy of emotion. As they come down, springing lightly on their stiffened legs, both birds touch the surface with their bills, scooping water over themselves in a sweeping sidewise motion.

At the high point of their leap they throw their heads back, arching their necks so that the bills point skyward. The wings flap in a flowing, graceful rhythm. The legs are stiff and straight, so that they act like springs, sending the birds bouncing upward again and again like two people on pogo sticks. When they strike the ground at the end of a series of jumps, they run toward each other, nodding their heads very gravely and flapping their huge wings. Then more leaps. Once the male, in a tremendous spring, jumped clear over the female, turning almost completely around as he was coming down.

The climax is an exhausting series of bounding leaps, an almost frantic effort, and then, as suddenly as it began, the dance is over. On another occasion, I saw the male continue his leaps solo, bounding off across the pond for some distance, the female walking away as if she had had enough. Throughout these performances the young crane watches in a bewildered manner at first, and then resumes his feeding as if completely bored by the whole business.

As the winter season moves on, a definite change takes place in the relationship of parents and young. When the dances of the adults have become an almost daily occurrence, so that for certain periods in the day the pair are more or less preoccupied with them and with each other, it is time for the weaning of the youngster. By now the young crane has lost nearly all of the buff and rusty feathers of his extreme youth and from a distance appears entirely white and indistinguishable from an adult, although at close range you can see remnants of his immaturity. The proud regard of his parents, especially the tender care of the mother, has been such an unwavering flame that it must come as a decided shock to him when she abruptly turns on him one day and, with head lowered in the attacking posture, runs at him and sends him flapping off in frightened bewilderment. It is time to break the tie, to cut him loose from her apron! The youngster is driven off again and again, for he can't believe it's true. At length, accepting this new state of things, he sulks on his own pasture, finding his own tidbits, as he is now perfectly capable of doing.

Nevertheless, with this lesson learned, he is at length permitted to return to the family precincts, though on a different basis. And from time to time he must be reminded of his new status. For the day of departure draws near. You can see it in the restless movements of the birds themselves, and almost feel the urgency of it in the air. And when they take to the upper reaches at last, and wheel magnificently until they find the course, the young crane will journey with them. The busy winter will then be over, and with spring and the long voyage northward, a new chapter is opened, and with it will come new scenes, new dangers, and new hopes.

FROM *On the Trail of Vanishing Birds*

The Origin of the Threat Postures

NIKO TINBERGEN

Careful observation and scientific discipline, as in the work of Niko Tinbergen, Konrad Lorenz, and Edward Armstrong, has brought public attention to the behavior of birds. Their court-ship displays, their ritualized greetings, their nest building, their communal responses to light and dark, have strong feelings, often conflicting drives, behind them. Their ceremonial behavior is also part of the conventions of their societies and necessary for their survival and well-being.

☙

Anyone who studies "display" in animals, either threat display or courtship display, cannot help wondering why the animals adopt such special, and often grotesque, attitudes.

Such attitudes are usually very typical for the species, and they may be rather similar in related species, but they are often very different from one taxonomic group to another. In the last two decades, much work has been done on this problem, and we begin now, however dimly, to understand something of the origin of such displays. In the Herring Gull, I think we have made a definite step forward, and although the conclusions I here put forward may not apply to all other types of display, I think that they may help in understanding many of the types found in other animals.

. . . the [upright] threat posture . . . seems to be a preparation for actual attack. The main argument in favour of this view is that a very aggressive bird lifts its wings out of the supporting feathers and keeps them ready for action. The posture of neck and head provides another argument. The neck is stretched and the head pointed downward. This is exactly the attitude adopted by a gull before it delivers a peck at its opponent. In a real fight, a gull always tries to jump on top of its enemy, and then peck at it and/or deliver wing-blows. It can, therefore, be seen that several elements of this threat posture are incipient fight-movements. Such incipient movements, also called preparatory or intention movements, are known to every student of behaviour. They occur especially when a drive is not fully aroused. Before a bird (of any species) decides to fly off, for instance, it flattens its plumage, raises its wings, often bends in the heel-joints and, after that, stretches the body strongly in the direction of flight. With a growing intensity of the urge to fly (for instance when the disturbance which caused the bird's anxiety is approaching), the intention movement develops into real flight. . . . Daanje has recently shown how widespread is the occurrence of such intention movements in birds. I myself have studied this

type of behaviour more closely in the nest-building behaviour of the male Three-spined Stickleback. When a male
stickleback has just settled in its territory, the first signs of
nest-building are incipient digging movements. At first, the
male merely fixes the sandy bottom with both eyes, bending
downwards a little. Nothing more happens on this occasion,
and after about a second the male again assumes a horizontal position and swims on. A minute later, however, it may
again fixate the bottom, and bend down somewhat farther.
On the next occasion, it may bring its head down to the bottom, and may even touch it with its snout. With rising intensity of the drive, it will begin to thrust its snout into the
sand, and may even suck some sand into its mouth, only to
spit it out immediately. Next, it will bore its snout deep into
the soil, take a mouthful of sand, and carry it off a few
inches before throwing it out. When digging with complete
vigour, it may carry the sand away over a distance of ten
inches or more. The increase in intensity is not quite so regular as I describe it; there are irregular ups and downs, but
the general trend is an increase of intensity as sketched here.
One has only to read Eliot Howard's description of the beginning of nest-building in birds to recognise the close parallel.

Such intention movements are of great importance for
our understanding of an animal's motivation at a particular
moment; to the experienced watcher they reveal what drive
is activated in the animal, and therefore, what type of activity he can expect to see next. It requires much intensive
watching to be able to recognise these rudiments of movements, and the better one knows a species, the more trivial
are the clues which one can recognise with certainty. Each
time that I study a new species I am amazed to find how
much more I see after I have become thoroughly acquainted

with it. After more than ten years of close study of the Three-spined Stickleback, for instance, I notice that my ability to recognise intention movements in this species is still improving, thus leading to new discoveries each season, and causing me surprise, and a kind of annoyance about my own previous stupidity. For once you have discovered a new and subtle intention movement, you simply cannot understand how it was possible for you to overlook it before, although it must have been happening dozens of times right under your nose. This experience also works the other way round: it gives one very little confidence in the conclusions drawn by workers who have not spent at least several months in intensive watching of a species. I cannot help thinking that the man who does not have the patience simply to sit and watch for hours, days, and weeks, is not the type of man to undertake a behaviour-study.

FROM *The Herring Gull's World*

The Aesthetic Sense

KARL VON FRISCH

Karl Von Frisch, a forerunner in the modern science of ecology, is well known for his discovery of the way bees communicate. His book about them is entitled The Dancing Bees. *He was awarded the Nobel Prize in 1973 for his pioneering studies in animal behavior.*

Satin bowerbirds build hutlike nests resembling human habitations, and decorate little avenues in front of them with blue and yellow flowers, blue berries, and blue glass beads to match their blue eyes. This seems to belong to a fantasy land which does not fit the world of birds as most of us know it. The courtship behavior of bowerbirds, as described here by Von Frisch, displays architectural skill and a remarkable sense of color which might arouse human envy. But this points less to an accident of evolution than to the development in this group of birds of a sense of proportion, allied to their sense of color. The inner feelings of birds in general often display complex affinities with this creative earth for which we have hardly started to give them credit.

✒

The Satin Bowerbird

The satin bowerbird (*Ptilonorhynchus violaceus*) lives in the rain forests of eastern Australia. The male, which is about the size of a pigeon, starts building his bower long before the onset of the mating season, and chooses for it a not too shaded spot on the forest floor. First, he clears all debris from an area of ground about one meter square. Next, he makes a kind of avenue by sticking bunches of straight twigs, twenty to thirty centimeters long, into the ground in two parallel rows. At the southern end, where most light will penetrate in the course of a day, he prepares a dancing floor, putting down a carpet of fine twigs and grass. He then collects bright objects to decorate it. He prefers dark blue and yellow-green colors, possibly because the blue ones match the bluish-violet radiance of his plumage, and the yellow-green ones resemble both the yellow-green color of his beak when fully mature and the yellow-green plumage of the female. He decorates the bower with blue and yellow flowers, blue-colored berries, and parrots' feathers. Where he is near human habitations, he adds to his display such products of our civilization as glass beads and strands of colored wool and tinsel. But this is by no means all. He actually paints the inside of his bower with the juice of the blue berries that he crushes in his beak. Sometimes he even uses a tool for the purpose. He picks up a piece of fibrous bark simultaneously with a squashed berry and proceeds to use the bark, soaked in the juice of the berry, like a brush or sponge.

Though the bower itself is finished in a few days, the bird's work does not end there. He constantly removes withered flowers and dried-up berries, replaces them with fresh ones, and generally adds to his collection as much as he can. In this he is completely unscrupulous: he steals from neighboring bowers if their owners happen to be away. When some pieces of blue-colored glass were placed on a suitable spot by an ornithologist, they were eagerly carried away, and soon they appeared in all the bowers of the district. As the pieces had each been marked with a number, it was not too difficult to trace their migrations from one bower to another as a result of constant multilateral thieving. Maintenance, too, is a laborious task. The heavy tropical rains damage the bowers, wash off the paint, and necessitate repairs. Preparations may thus keep a bird busy over many weeks.

When mating time approaches, the cock redoubles his efforts to attract the attention of a female to his bower and display by intoning a raucous courtship song. Bowerbirds do not excel as singers. But some species adopt a highly personal form of acoustic wooing by imitating other sounds with amazing fidelity, be it the song of other birds or the roll of thunder.

If a female has come to his bower, the male gets more and more excited as he tries to win her. He hops around the bower, dances on the place in front, and constantly picks up various ornaments with his beak to show them to his visitor. His excitement enables him to produce a very special effect: he can change the pale blue of his iris into a dark, bluish-violet hue matching his plumage, a color which is so markedly preferred in his exterior and interior decoration. Courtship play continues until at last the female shows her willingness, slips into the arbor, and mates with him. . . .

The Orange-Crested Gardener

The measures taken by the male to attract the attention of a female and the courtship displays designed to win her favor are probably most highly developed in another group of this fascinating family. I choose the orange-crested gardener (*Amblyornis subalaris*) as my example. It is a bird the size of a starling, with inconspicuous plumage, which lives in the dark, inaccessible mountain forests of New Guinea. At mating time, the male builds a little hut on the forest floor. I use the word "hut" advisedly, because it really is a hut with a rainproof roof, with a circular passage inside designed for a tryst, and a colorful mosaic between the two openings. In front of this structure, there is a well-tended garden strewn with flowers and separated from the surrounding area by a fence richly decorated with yellow and red fruit. A. P. Goodwin, the first author to report on their bowers, described these creations as the most beautiful objects ever constructed by birds. His view remains valid today.

As with the Lauterbach bowerbirds, the bowers were known, but all efforts to watch the birds at work or observe their courtship displays remained fruitless for a long time. Even Sielmann nearly failed, despite his determination. With the aid of experienced local helpers, he finally managed to penetrate to the courtship area. There, in a cleverly constructed hide, he and his assistants waited endlessly with their cameras for a chance to film. But under a constantly overcast sky, the light in the dark rain forest was insufficient for his purpose. At long last, after weeks of waiting in the hot and clammy hide, their patience was rewarded. An occasional ray of sun penetrated the dense canopy, allowing them to record on film events that seemed almost incredible.

When the party had first arrived, the hut of the orange-crested gardener had already been completed. But heavy downpours played havoc with it, and they could repeatedly watch the bird restoring order to house and garden. The dome-shaped roof of the hut, made of densely interwoven twigs, had not suffered, as it was built around the stem of a sapling for support. The front side of this stem, or center column, was covered with a thick layer of very dark green moss. It is the habit of the orange-crested gardener to place the treasures of his collection on the dark moss in the manner of a jeweler exhibiting his wares on a ground of dark velvet for better effect, and here the bird had much work to do after each heavy rainstorm. He insisted on perfect order and regularity. To the left, there would be a collection of glittering blue beetles; to the right, the shiny fragments of broken snail shells; both groups were separated from each other by a line of yellow flowers. All this was meticulously arranged and stuck into the moss at carefully chosen intervals.

FROM *Animal Architecture*

The Light-Mantled
Sooty Albatross

LOUIS J. HALLE

Louis J. Halle, author of Spring in Washington *and* Owl of
Athena, *is also known for his writing on international affairs
and political philosophy.*

*In the following passage, this civilized, acute observer of
birds speculates about a manifestation of nature that has
reached a state of perfection and artistry seemingly beyond human achievement. The albatross flies out of the primal depths
of creation.*

🐦

Leaving the Royal Albatrosses and turning right to descend
the slope of the hill obliquely, we marched down into a
draw and on up the other side of it toward the peak of Mt.

Lyall (1,355 feet). The slope got steep toward the top, where some volcanic scree led to a series of short stepped cliffs. On one of the first steps, merely a narrow ledge clothed in grass and fern, was a fantastic bird on a grass nest built up into a truncated cone. This was the Light-mantled Sooty Albatross, a bird of shades and shadings rather than black and white. The dark bill was comparatively thin and elegant. The forepart of the head was almost black, shading behind and down the neck to what became a most delicate light gray on the back and underparts. The wings folded against its flanks were a medium gray, and all deepened into sooty dark toward the tail. Most references to nature as an artist are mere cant, but there are occasions when one is suddenly struck by the fact that it is so in a profound sense. Surely this fantastic bird is the product of something more than the mere utility that is the basis of natural selection.

What, one may ask, does the work of a Picasso have to do with the work of a blind process like natural selection? The question is pertinent, because this bird on its nest is more plausible as the product of the former than of the latter. (There are philosophical implications here, if we would only apply our minds to them.)

This elegant bird greeted us, as we climbed up to its pedestal, like the royalty we had just left, by bill-clapping. Because its more delicate bill made less noise, however, the clapping had to be supplemented by grunts. Like the Royal Albatross, it closed its bill on Crompton's arm when he put his hand under its body to draw out and check on the egg.

FROM *The Sea and the Ice: A Naturalist in Antarctica*

The Kingfisher

TED HUGHES

*The belted kingfisher of North America is not as brilliantly col-
ored as the European kingfisher, the subject of Ted Hughes's
poem, which follows. But it is a bird of striking appearance,
with a crest on its large head, blue-green and chestnut feathers,
and a stout bill with which it catches its prey. In his* Birds of
Massachusetts, *Edward Howe Forbush called it "this wild,
grotesque, tousled-headed bird." It is a superior fisherman,
flying with rattling cry off the water to its perch, under blue-
gray skies as soft as its own plumage. The female is unusual
among birds in that with a rust-colored band around her belly,
she seems to be more dressed up than the male. Among the La-
kota, anyone who dreamed of the belted kingfisher* (hoyazela)
*was made a bird doctor. In Chinese poetry "kingfisher blue"
and "kingfisher green" often appear. This bird has long attracted our sense of the miraculous.*

The scientific name for the belted kingfisher is Megaceryle alcyon. *The word "halcyon," as applied to the kingfisher, stems from the Greek* alkuon, *and was connected with an ancient fable that the bird bred during the winter solstice on a floating nest. It was said to be able to charm the turbulent winter wind and the waves so that the sea calmed down. Hence "halcyon days" are days when the waters are calm and blue.*

The Kingfisher perches. He studies.

Escaped from the jeweller's opium
X-rays the river's toppling
Tangle of glooms.

Now he's vanished—into vibrations.
A sudden electric wire, jarred rigid,
Snaps—with a blue flare.

He has left his needle buried in your ear.

Oafish oaks, kneeling, bend over
Dragging with their reflections
For the sunken stones. The Kingfisher
Erupts through the mirror, a shower of prisms—

A spilling armful of gems, beak full of ingots,
And is away—cutting the one straight line
Of the raggle-taggle tumbledown river
With a diamond—

Leaves a rainbow splinter sticking in your eye.

Through him, God, whizzing in the sun,
Glimpses the angler.

Through him, God
Marries a pit
Of fishy mire.

        And look! He's
—gone again.

        Spark, sapphire, refracted
From beyond water
Shivering the spine of the river.

FROM *The River*

Part Four

Birds and the American Land

In her book *The Land of Little Rain,* Mary Austin wrote about a land that most people still think of as inhospitable, arid, and uninviting. We "overcome" the desert, in the same way that we overcame much of the continent. The native people, who had lived with the desert for thousands of years before the white men showed up, knew its secrets: the hidden ways, for example, of the plants that supplied them with food. The birds, as well as all the desert's original inhabitants, were actors, part of a long enduring story. The birds were winged messengers from a symbolic universe of primal directions, relived every day and night under the great sun and the stars. The desert, Austin wrote, is a region in which plants and animals are "cheerfully adapted to seasonal limitations." Later writers like Joseph Wood Krutch have found that to live in the desert leads to enlightenment of a rare kind and offers insights we can never attain without going there.

The land we call American is not entirely understood, even by modern nature writers and natural scientists. Any distinct range encompasses a complex of associated life, all responding to a very ancient past. The New World was not new because we named it so. Nor can we really understand so varied a race as the birds, with all their attributes, outside the context of the land, the sea, the air above us. We will never know birds well enough—and the writers included here understand this—without respecting the universal equality they share with us. Nor can we approach them without realizing that we do not know the land either, unless we see it in more than our own manipulative terms. Modern science is not enough. We have to go back again to the land we started with.

Where the Birds
Are Our Friends

GARY PAUL NABHAN

Gary Nabhan, the naturalist writer, ethnobiologist, and au-thority on desert plants, wrote The Desert Smells Like Rain, *from which the following extract is taken. It speaks to how birds and people can coexist, when neither has been brought in only to view the other.*

❧

Bob Thomas of the *Arizona Republic* later commented on the Park Service's superficial commitment to its mandate of preserving ". . . various objects of historic and scientific in-terest." In a 1967 article entitled "Price of Progress Comes High," Thomas wrote:

. . . Near Quitobaquito on the Organ Pipe National Monument a few years ago a government bulldozer knocked down the home of the late José Juan, a Papago Indian who lived there all his life. In doing so, workmen churned up the only known stratification of human habitation between Ajo and Yuma.

He added that the Papago:

. . . distrust the government's promises to protect the park's treasures. In the past, the government has unknowingly or unfeelingly destroyed historic and prehistoric artifacts in the area.

By this destruction, the Park Service gained a bird sanctuary to provide tourists with a glimpse of wild plants and animals that gather around a desert water source.

Or so they thought. For an odd thing is happening at their "natural" bird sanctuary. They are losing the heterogeneity of the habitat, and with it, the birds. The old trees are dying. Few new ones are being regenerated. There are only three cottonwoods left, and four willows. These riparian trees are essential for the breeding habitat of certain birds. Summer annual seedplants are conspicuously absent from the pond's surroundings. Without the soil disturbance associated with plowing and flood irrigation, these natural foods for birds and rodents no longer germinate.

Visiting *A'al Waipia* and *Ki:towak* on back-to-back days three times during one year, ornithologists accompanying me encountered more birds at the Papago village than at the "wildlife sanctuary." Overall, we identified more than sixty-five species at the Papago's *Ki:towak,* and less than thirty-two at the Park Service's *A'al Waipia.* As Dr. Amadeo Rea put it, "It is as if someone fired a shotgun just before we

arrived there. The conspicuous absences were more reveal-
ing than what we actually encountered."

When I explained to Remedio that we were finding far
fewer birds and plants at the uninhabited oasis, he grew in-
trospective. Finally, the Papago farmer had to speak:

"I've been thinking over what you say about not so many
birds living over there anymore. That's because those birds,
they come where the people are. When the people live and
work in a place, and plant their seeds and water their trees,
the birds go live with them. They like those places, there's
plenty to eat and that's when we are friends to them."

I think that Remedio would even argue that it is natural
for birds to cluster at human habitations, around fields and
fencerows. I'll go even further. It's in a sense natural for
desert-dwelling humans over the centuries to have gathered
around the *A'al Waipia* and *Ki:towak* oases. And although
they didn't keep these places as pristine wilderness environments—an Anglo-American expectation of parks in the
West—the Papago may have increased their biological di-
versity.

So if you're ever down in Organ Pipe Cactus National
Monument and visit the Park Service wildlife sanctuary of
Quitobaquito, remember that an old Papago place called
A'al Waipia lies in ruin there. Its spirit is alive, less than forty
miles away, in a true Sonoran Desert oasis. There, the ir-
rigation ditches are filled with tules, and they radiate out
from the pond into the fields like a green sunburst.
Ki:towak.

FROM *The Desert Smells Like Rain:
A Naturalist in Papago Indian Country*

Bird Neighbors:
The Bluebird

JOHN BURROUGHS

Modern, illustrated field guides are indispensable, for beginners as well as professionals. Still, they do not describe the character of a bird or, in anything but an abbreviated form, its habitat. The birds are not treated as neighbors, perhaps for the good reason that we have to make a concerted effort in our urbanized society to go out and find them.

John James Audubon and, later, Edward Howe Forbush and Arthur Cleveland Bend, lived at a time when the countryside was much richer in bird life than it is today. As a result, their bird biographies and life histories have been indispensable to later ornithologists and writers in the field. They were based on taking time. Naturalists of an earlier period, when farm and countryside still reigned, not only gave you statistics, they provided stories and descriptions. It is not to detract from the greater convenience of a field guide to say that while it identifies a life, it does not help the reader very much to relate to it.

John Burroughs, a prolific writer, had a great enthusiasm for all the local birds he saw during his life. His books attracted a variety of people who wanted to know more about their own localities. His comfortable, familiar treatment of wild birds also characterizes the style of Edward Howe Forbush in his three-volume Birds of Massachusetts. He collected a vast amount of information and observations on the 286 species he included in those books. One of his purposes, in addition to public education, was "rational conservation," because the decline of the birds had become increasingly obvious.

Forbush not only included all the knowledgeable detail that was available to him, he also took much pleasure in telling stories about his subjects, and he was not stingy with his adjectives. The hummingbird is a "mighty warrior"; the great horned owl is "the most morose, savage and saturnine of the New England birds"; the chickadee is "self confident." He was also not ashamed of adding certain homely observations, which for reasons of scientific accuracy, might not be tolerated today. Although with a mild disclaimer, he puts in an assertion by Thomas Nuttall that the raven, that "dour, sombre" bird, "has been seen in the midst of a thunderstorm with the electric fluid streaming from the end of his bill, a statement that may be doubted by the sceptic." He describes a loon flying through a gale at sea with delight, as if he were there in person.

⇗

And yonder bluebird with the earth tinge on his breast and the sky tinge on his back,—did he come down out of heaven on that bright March morning when he told us so softly and plaintively that, if we pleased, spring had come? Indeed, there is nothing in the return of the birds more curious and suggestive than in the first appearance, or rumors of the appearance, of this little blue-coat. The bird at first seems a mere wandering voice in the air: one hears its call or carol on some bright March morning, but is uncertain of its source or direction; it falls like a drop of rain when no cloud is visible; one looks and listens, but to no purpose. The weather changes, perhaps a cold snap with snow comes on, and it may be a week before I hear the note again, and this time or the next perchance see the bird sitting on a stake in the fence lifting his wing as he calls cheerily to his mate. Its notes now become daily more frequent; the birds multiply, and, flitting from point to point, call and warble more confidently and gleefully. Their boldness increases till one sees them hovering with a saucy, inquiring air about barns and outbuildings, peeping into dove-cotes and stable windows, inspecting knotholes and pump-trees, intent only on a place to nest. They wage war against robins and wrens, pick quarrels with swallows, and seem to deliberate for days over the policy of taking forcible possession of one of the mud-houses of the latter. But as the season advances they drift more into the background. Schemes of conquest which they at first seemed bent upon are abandoned, and they settle down very quietly in their old quarters in remote stumpy fields.

FROM *Wake-Robin*

Bird Neighbors:
The Eastern Screech Owl

FRANK M. CHAPMAN

The Screech Owl frequently makes its home near our dwellings and sometimes selects a convenient nook in them in which to lay its eggs. But its favorite retreat is an old apple orchard, where the hollow limbs offer it a secure refuge from the mobs of small birds which are ever ready to attack it. A search in the trees of an orchard of this kind rarely fails to result in the discovery of one or more of these feathered inhabitants who may have resided there for years. They attempt to escape capture by a show of resistance and a castanetlike cracking of the bill, but when brought from their hiding-place sit quietly, dazzled for a moment by the sudden light. They then elongate themselves and almost close their eyes, thus rendering themselves as inconspicuous as possible. How differently they appear when the western sky fades and *their* day begins! Is any bird more thoroughly awake than a hungry Screech Owl? With ear-tufts erected, and his great, round eyes opened to the utmost, he is the picture of alertness.

When night comes, one may hear the Screech Owl's tremulous, wailing whistle. It is a weird, melancholy call, welcomed only by those who love Nature's voice whatever be the medium through which she speaks.

FROM *Handbook of Birds of Eastern North America*

Bird Neighbors: The Golden-Crowned Kinglet

ARTHUR CLEVELAND BENT

Many years ago, a boy found on the doorstep the body of a tiny feathered gem. Perhaps the cat had left it there, but, as it was a bitter, cold morning in midwinter, it is more likely that it had perished with the cold and hunger. He picked it up and was entranced with the delicate beauty of its soft olive colors and with its crown of brilliant orange and gold, which glowed like a ball of fire. In his eagerness to preserve it, he attempted to make his first birdskin. It made a sorry-looking specimen, but it was the beginning of a life-long interest in birds, which has lasted for over a half century. Since then many a winter landscape in southern New England has been enlivened by the cheery little groups of kinglets, wandering through our evergreen woods, bravely facing winter's storms and cold, for it is only at that season that we are likely to see them south of the Canadian Zone.

The summer home is in the coniferous forests of the northern tier of States and in the southern Provinces of Canada. Ora W. Knight says that, in Maine, "pine, fir, spruce and hemlock woods, or mixed growth in which these trees predominate are their preference." Most observers say that they prefer the spruces. William Brewster found them breeding in Winchendon, Mass., in dense woods of white pine and spruce. Based on my limited experience, golden-crowned kinglets seem to prefer the more open forests of more or less scattered, second-growth spruces, rather than the dense forests of mature growth. In these more open forests there are often a few balsam firs or white birches scattered through the spruces, but the presence of spruces seems to be necessary for nesting purposes.

In the Adirondack Mountains of New York, according to Aretas A. Saunders, this kinglet "lives in the coniferous forests, especially in the tops of tall spruces. Spruce, hemlock, balsam, and tamarack all attract it, and it is seldom seen in summer in the hardwoods, and then only where spruces are near. On the Avalanche Pass Trail I found it in second growth spruce, where the trees were dense but only ten or fifteen feet high."

FROM *Life Histories of North American Thrushes,*
Kinglets and Their Allies

Bird Neighbors:
The Black-Capped Chickadee

EDWARD HOWE FORBUSH

The little Black-capped Chickadee is the embodiment of cheerfulness, verve and courage. It can boast no elegant plumes, and it makes no claims as a songster, yet this blithe woodland sprite is a distinctive character, and is a bird masterpiece beyond all praise. It is spruce and smart in its plain black, gray and white livery; and its cheery, cordial notes are the "open sesame" to woodland secrets. Follow the call of a Chickadee and it will introduce you to its brethren and to a sociable gathering of kinglets, nuthatches, a Downy Woodpecker or two, and possibly a creeper. In the proper seasons migrating warblers may also join the group. A born leader is this little "scrap of valor." The other birds seem to know that Chickadee's superior intelligence and prying eyes will guide them to places where insect food is most abundant.

Let the north winds howl, let the snowstorm rage—it may be bitter cold, but Chickadee worries not as he hustles about to keep his little stomach filled with insects. Only the ice storm which envelops the trees and conceals the insects beneath its crystal cloak is likely to have an intimidating effect on Chickadee's otherwise deep-rooted self-confidence. Then it will come to human friends for food and care, or else hie away to some snug refuge in a hollow limb or deserted bird's nest, there to abide till the storm has run its course.

At this season Chickadees are the prevailing birds, and one usually finds them roving the woods in small bands. Move quietly now; imitate their *"phe-be"* call, or suck in gently on the back of your hand, which will give rise to low, squeaky sounds. This ruse will not fail to attract our little friends, for they are innately inquisitive. Soon they flit and flutter about the twigs right over your head, come close at arm's length and peer down at you with their keen bead-like eyes and scold you or mock you with a voluble chattering of *chic-chic-a-dee-dee.* If you are patient and still, perhaps one or more of these bold birds will want to satisfy its curiosity by alighting on some part of you, when you will experience "the thrill of a lifetime." Dr. Frank M. Chapman writes of such encounters—"On several occasions Chickadees have flown down and perched upon my hand. During the few seconds they remained there I became rigid with the emotion of this novel experience. It was a mark of confidence which seemed to initiate me into the ranks of woodland dwellers."

FROM *Birds of Massachusetts and Other New England States*

Bird Neighbors:
The Loon; Or,
Great Northern Diver

EDWARD HOWE FORBUSH

The Loon is a wonderful, powerful, living mechanism fashioned for riding the stormy seas. See him as he mounts high
above the waves, neck and legs fully extended "fore and
aft," and bill a trifle raised which gives to his whole form a
slight upward bend, his wings beating powerfully and moving as steadily as the walking-beam of a side-wheel steam-
ship. He is driving straight ahead into the teeth of the gale
and making greater headway than the laboring steamer that
steers a parallel course. Now he slants downward, and striking just beyond the top of a towering wave shoots down its
inclined surface and rises again on the coming crest. Here,
midway of the wide bay where the seas are running high

and wildly tossing their white tops, with a wintry gale whipping the spray from them in smoky gusts, the Loon rests at ease, head to the wind and sea like a ship at anchor. The tossing and the tumult disturb him not, as he rides, light as a birch canoe, turning up his white breast now and then on one side as he reaches unconcernedly backward to preen his feathers. His neck narrows at the water-line into a beautifully modeled cutwater. His broad paddles push his white breast to the tops of the great waves, where it parts the foam as he surmounts the crests and glides easily down into the gulfs beyond. The freezing spray that loads the fishing fleet with tons of ice seems never to cling to his tough and glossy plumage; or if it does, he washes it off among the fleeing fishes away down in the warmer currents near the bottom of the bay.

Often toward nightfall I have heard his wild storm-call far out to windward against the black pall of an approaching tempest like the howl of a lone wolf coming down the wind; and have seen his white breast rise on a wave against the black sky to vanish again like the arm of a swimmer lost in the stormy sea. Sailors, hearing the call, say that the loons are trying to blow up an "easterly." At times his cries seem wailing and sad as if he were bemoaning his exile from his forest lake. Such is the Loon in his winter home off our coast; for there he lives and braves the inclemency of the season. Of all the wild creatures that persist in New England, the Loon seems best to typify the stark wildness of primeval nature.

FROM *Birds of Massachusetts and Other New England States*

Bartram and the Birds

WILLIAM BARTRAM

These two bird descriptions are taken from William Bartram's classic Travels, *first published in Philadelphia in 1791. His graphic account records that his travels took him through what was then sparsely inhabited wilderness, now the "Deep South" states from the Carolinas to Florida. His narrative style, rich in imagery, inspired writers from Coleridge to Emerson.*

⤳

The Wild Turkey

I saw here a remarkably large turkey of the native wild breed; his head was above three feet from the ground when he stood erect; he was a stately beautiful bird, of a very dark dusky brown colour, the tips of the feathers of his neck, breast, back, and shoulders, edged with a copper colour, which in a certain exposure looked like burnished gold, and he seemed not insensible of the splendid appearance he made. He was reared from an egg, found in the forest, and hatched by a hen of the common domestic fowl.

Our turkey of America is a very different species from the meleagris of Asia and Europe; they are nearly thrice their size and weight. I have seen several that have weighed between twenty and thirty pounds, and some have been killed that weighed near forty. They are taller, and have a much longer neck proportionally, and likewise longer legs, and stand more erect; they are also very different in colour. Ours are all, male and female, of a dark brown colour, not having a black feather on them; but the male exceedingly splendid, with changeable colours. In other particulars they differ not. . . . Having rested very well during the night, I was awakened in the morning early, by the cheering converse of the wild turkeycocks (Meleagris occidentalis) saluting each other, from the sun-brightened tops of the lofty Cupressus disticha and Magnolia grandiflora. They begin at early dawn, and continue till sun-rise, from March to the last of April. The high forests ring with the noise, like the crowing of the domestic cock, of these social centinels; the watch-word being caught and repeated, from one to another, for hundreds of miles around; insomuch that the whole country is for an hour or more in an universal shout. A little after sun-rise, their crowing gradually ceases, they quit their high lodging-places, and alight on the earth, where expanding their silver bordered train, they strut and dance round about the coy female, while the deep forests seem to tremble with their shrill noise.

The Snake Bird; Or, American Anhinga

Here is in this river, and in the waters all over Florida, a very curious and handsome species of birds, the people call them Snake Birds; I think I have seen paintings of them on the Chinese screens and other India pictures: they seem to

be a species of cormorant or loon (Colymbus cauda elon-
gata), but far more beautiful and delicately formed than any
other species that I have ever seen. The head and neck of
this bird are extremely small and slender, the latter very
long indeed, almost out of all proportion; the bill long,
straight, and slender, tapering from its ball to a sharp point;
all the upper side, the abdomen and thighs, are as black and
glossy as a raven's, covered with feathers so firm and elastic,
that they in some degree resemble fish-scales; the breast and
upper part of the belly are covered with feathers of a cream
colour; the tail is very long, of a deep black, and tipped with
a silvery white, and when spread, represents an unfurled
fan. They delight to sit in little peaceable communities, on
the dry limbs of trees, hanging over the still waters, with
their wings and tails expanded, I suppose to cool and air
themselves, when at the same time they behold their images
in the watery mirror. At such times, when we approach
them, they drop off the limbs into the water as if dead, and
for a minute or two are not to be seen; when on a sudden,
at a vast distance, their long slender head and neck only appear, and have very much the appearance of a snake, and
no other part of them is to be seen when swimming in the
water, except sometimes the tip end of the tail. In the heat
of the day they are seen in great numbers, sailing very high
in the air, over lakes and rivers.

I doubt not but if this bird had been an inhabitant of the
Tiber in Ovid's days, it would have furnished him with a
subject for some beautiful and entertaining metamorpho-
ses. I believe it feeds intirely on fish, for its flesh smells and
tastes intolerably strong of it; it is scarcely to be eaten, unless
constrained by insufferable hunger.

FROM *The Travels of William Bartram*

Birds Sowing and Harvesting

TED LEVIN

In the following passage from his book, Blood Brook, *a contemporary naturalist in Vermont follows in the tradition of earlier writers who were keen observers of the plants and animals in their own neighborhood.*

୬

It is birds, birds with tastes very close to my own, that propagate shrubs and trees all across the valley. Cedar waxwings, robins, bluebirds, catbirds, veerys, wood thrushes, and hermit thrushes are so indispensable to berry bushes—and consequently and inadvertently to my family's summer happiness—that the plants' fruiting strategy integrates the birds' need for food and the plants' need for seed dispersal.

Waxwings prize Blood Brook blueberries and strawberries. They hop up from the unmowed lawn, their bills stained red, and fly to a maple limb to digest the sweet flesh of the fruit. The seeds pass unharmed through their intestines, then are defecated at some distance from its parent plant. This movement benefits the plant for two reasons. First, any seed germinating beneath the parent plant has to compete for light, water, and nutrients with mature members of its own species, plants whose roots are deeper, branches longer, and leaves fuller and more numerous than those of a germinating seedling. Second, because bird-dispersed seeds are scattered in small numbers, they are less likely to be eaten by seed-eating white-footed mice, which forage where seeds are numerous.

Casey, who celebrates his birthday at the height of the strawberry season, knows the waxwing only as a competitor. Someday he may appreciate that, like succession itself, the relationship between bird and berry and boy is circular.

To attract local seed dispersers and to cut down on wasted seed production (unpicked fruits rot on the stem or fall to the ground and become available to mice), some plants show preripening fruit flags; that is, the fruits go through a double color change before they mature. Green at first, such fruits become pink or red before turning a final color. Blueberries and blackberries turn pink before ripening; strawberries turn white, catching the eye of resident fruit-eating birds (and boys), alerting them to the imminent availability of ripe fruit. Some autumn-ripening fruits advertise their presence by leaf color. The leaves of wild grape, Virginia creeper, and poison ivy, vines that climb the trunks of deciduous trees along Blood Brook, change color to red and yellow about the time fall thrushes pass through the valley while the rest of the woods are still green. Like

highway billboards, these colored leaves direct hungry migrants . . . to sources of fast food; like harried tourists, these
travelers do not have the time and energy, or familiarity
with the local landscape, to search for their next meal.

The sequential ripening of fruits coincides with the energy demands of local or migrant birds. Summer fruits such
as Juneberry, strawberry, blueberry, black raspberry, and
blackberry are all high in carbohydrates and are eaten by
resident birds. Fatty fruits such as the poison ivy berry ripen
in the fall and are consumed for the most part by migratory
birds, which need its high-lipid contents to fuel their migration. High-lipid fruits decompose faster than low-lipid
fruits and must be eaten, if their seeds are to be dispersed,
as soon as they ripen. Fall fruits that are high in carbohydrates and low in lipids, such as sumac, barberry, wild rai-
sin, crab apple, and highbush cranberry, are bypassed by the
migrants and remain on the plant for most of the winter.
Slow to decay, they will be available to wintering birds and
early spring migrants.

Sumac, the driest, fuzziest, least inviting fruit that I
know, scorned all winter by scores of birds, becomes a
March staple for pine grosbeaks and robins that, like kids,
have eaten the more palatable foods first. These birds ex-
ercise their preferences through fall and winter, but, inevitably, if reluctantly, come to sumac in March, in a self-
sustaining system that rewards producer and consumer, as
well as observer.

FROM *Blood Brook*

Our Lads

JAKE PAGE

These two essays from Jake Page's book Songs to Birds *are samples of his eloquent tribute to some American birds. He is a modern day bird watcher of wit, learning, and enthusiasm. Among his other books are* Lords of the Air, *and* Hopi, *written in collaboration with his wife, Susanne, a photographer.*

❧

This is a story of a crime.

They arrived one July in a disreputable sprawl of skin and bone, clinging to a dark and sooty nest in the fireplace. *Chaetura pelagica,* chimney swifts—common enough arrivals in the affairs of human beings through some inefficiency of their species in fastening nests to the insides of chimneys. Featherless infants squalling for parental care, sounding like locusts. Four of them—one dead and the others more than likely doomed. The odds in life may be six-to-five against, but with orphaned baby birds the odds are infinitely worse.

As usual, Susanne went immediately to the rescue, plunging herself into the unknown exigencies of chimney swift motherhood. The creatures were gathered up, nasty nest and all, and put into a cardboard carton, while I headed for the bookshelf.

Insectivorous birds: Therefore the first step was to puree beef, add a touch of water and a little milk for calcium and, with an eyedropper, stick the puree into three open beaks. Chimney swifts are among the hardest bird orphans to feed because of their infernal head waggling. A miss here, a successful squirt there, and in a few minutes the screeching subsided. A chancy beginning.

Every hour they squalled and the puree was applied. Swifts fledge in thirty days. When did they hatch? Since they were featherless on arrival, we assume less than a week ago. Three weeks of dawn-to-dusk hourly feeding?

A few days passed and the birds began to show signs of feathers—follicles and fluff. The feathers came and the birds gained in size. I read up on the swifts. They are, like everything under the sun, wonderful beings, however little we know of their lives. Assuming for the moment that the babies survived, they would be capable of flight clocked up to thirty-five miles per hour. They would spend virtually all day in flight, soaring and swooping, batlike, after insects such as beetles and flying ants and airborne spiders. In the best of circumstances, these ragamuffin infants could live for fourteen years, during which time they could fly as many as a million and a half miles.

After a week, the babies' eyes opened and they stared at their mother with a total lack of expression, yelling for food. Imagine finding that your mother is about a thousand times bigger than you. An impossible standard.

Swifts are gregarious, roosting in groups of up to ten thousand, descending an hour after sunset into huge industrial chimneys like clouds of smoke in reverse action. They inhabit much of eastern North America in spring and summer, and winter in the upper Amazon basin in Brazil and Peru. Brazil? Peru?

This feeding is hopeless, we think. One gets its bill stuck shut, being sloppy with the puree. *Sturm und Drang* as warm water is applied. Another small crisis resolved. They continued to grow, turning sooty dark; short, stubby bills frowned at us, gibbety-gibbety, demanding. They traveled with us in the car as much as a hundred miles without protest.

When it was time for them to fledge, we learned, they would be able to fly across the room. We should then put them, the experts said, on a telephone pole. They'd climb to the top and take off. But where would they go at night? By even contemplating such questions, we realized we had reached the point where maybe the odds were only six-to-five against.

After about two more days, the swifts took to popping out of the wicker basket that early on had replaced their altogether disreputable hovel of a nest. They would hop onto Susanne's shirt, glaring like three upside-down bats, then climb upward into her blonde hair. Sharp, spiny tail feather tips stuck out like a comb, the swift's equivalent of a mountaineer's crampons. Little needles that could make you wince, but just the thing for clinging to the side of a chimney or to a surrogate mother.

Would they know about catching insects? Susanne swatted flies and occasionally substituted them, or mealworms, for the beef. They liked the beef better.

On the seventeenth day, Susanne bore them outdoors clinging to her shirt. It was a windy day, with the sun peering out between mountainous clouds. The birds climbed onto her head. They looked expressionlessly at the world. Overhead chimney swifts soared and swooped, along with barn swallows and purple martins. We thought it might do these preschoolers some good to have a glimpse of their ultimate role, but seeing the athletic grace going on overhead, we believed that there was no way our orphans would be equal to it.

At which point, one of the swifts, the one that had a suggestion of eagle in its countenance (or so we thought) and that had refused a morning meal that day, took off from Susanne's head. It flew low over our yard and the next, headed for a large tree, swerved, and sailed up into the clouded sky. The wild swifts gathered around, flying with it, soaring on scimitar wings. And our swift, flapping a bit frantically, took up its life in an altogether new medium, the sky, airborne, beautifully flying, among its own. We could pick it out because it appeared slightly larger (beef-fed, after all) and because it flew with its tail spread out, the novice sacrificing speed for security.

It flew. We cheered and hugged.

The swifts and their cousins circled the neighborhood, tiny dots high in the sky. And Susanne and I watched for more than an hour, wondering why no symphonic crescendo accompanied this event, then knowing there *was* such an accompaniment—the silent burst of our own joy and awe and, yes, pride. We knew that an inconsequential birdling was now at home, that the others would follow, engaged in majestic flight, and that as soon as they got their tails together, they would become anonymous members of their race, taking swift-type risks at swiftian odds. Soon, with any luck at all, they would be in the upper Amazon basin.

Under federal law, raising foundling birds of certain species is not legal unless you have a license. We don't. But criminal as our act was, we now vicariously share the feeling of flight—a parental feeling if you will. And every summer for several years now we have been able to look into the clouds and say, "Hey, those are our birds!"

And each spring, we think again of the gift we received from those sooty little birds: a direct connection with one of those great and mysterious cycles of the planet.

FROM *Songs to Birds*

Duck Weather

JAKE PAGE

Day One: Chincoteague, Virginia.

Rain. Rain that would unnerve Noah. Even the dry places in the marshlands of the Atlantic Coast fill up with water—pine needle puddles, brand new canals reflecting in a rain-pocked chaos the unnaturally dark sky.

West of here, in the Piedmont and beyond, there is snow, freezing rain, sleet, all those tiresome products of the wintry midwest where, perhaps from living with a big sky for too many generations, the people take such things for granted, perhaps even enjoying the martyrdom, the frontier spirit, of a massive March snow. Here, at least, near the sea where the laws of physics embodied in the Atlantic moderate the climate, it only rains.

Good weather for ducks, goes the old saw. Haw, haw. But it is not apparent that the ducks like this weather any more than the bird-watchers and other hobbyists who ply the rim of the marsh in their cars, keeping dry on the as-

phalt margin between wetland and pine woods. Through
the rain one hears the crash of the surf, improperly loud
inasmuch as the Midwestern storm blows eastward. Out beyond their brown perimeters of grass, turned copper by the
rain just as the pale lichens on the pine boles glow green,
the waters host little visible in the way of ducks and geese.
A pair of shovelers dutifully shovel along in the shallows.
A hundred yards farther out, widgeons widge forlornly. A
few Brant geese huddle near the shore, and here and there,
along the channels, crouching great blue herons glower at
their formerly promising territories.

Fog arises as the rains temporarily calm down. Islands of
Phragmites grass, scrubby myrtle shrubs, and a loblolly pine
or two emerge, only to disappear in the changing mist. Sky,
water, and land are one in the vapor—all is obscurity, still-
ness. The only mobile form of life visible is a mystery gull,
undeterred from some irritable duty, whomping along into
and out of view. The world might easily end in grey.

Day two.

A clear sky, whipped into purity by a wind from the
northwest. Diamonds glint from the vast expanses of water.
The loblolly pines and the myrtle bushes are full of little
grey birds—neither a flock nor a community, but a host—
flitting here and there, up, down, back and forth, chipping
high-pitched chips. Is this their normal manner or is it a
case of the observer observed? They are myrtle warblers,
named such for their preference for the berries of the myrtle
bushes so prevalent around the marsh. Every birder has seen
them; they are the most numerous warbler in the east. No
big deal, but it is pleasant to walk along and have them
dance before me.

Out in the water, a group of ten shovelers proceeds with
dignity. Who appoints the token shovelers on a day of fog

and rain? Where do the malingerers hunker down for a day
off? Widgeons in discreet couples, and pintails, make their
genteel way through the water, as do the black ducks.

The wind gusts unpredictably across the light sky-blue
shallows, darkening their surface in evanescent brush
strokes. A new artist at work here today. Beyond the shallow water, the brown cord grass is bent every which way,
an unkempt hairdo in need of a brush. The wind does its
best to achieve order, but the scalp of this place will before
long sprout new green hair, more amenable to training.
Dead grass rattles quietly in the wind.

A great heron looks imperiously at its domain, then dis-
dainfully at an approaching observer, and lifts into the
wind, ritually tucking its head back on its shoulders, and
leaves. Noblesse oblige.

Most of the swans and geese have left for the north. Except for a few teal, most of the spring migrants are still well
to the south. There are a few exceptions to the casual, even
bored, activities of the regulars. Two otters do a snake dance
in the water, like Nessie, and discreetly vanish behind a
hummock of grass to dally unflagrantly. Red-breasted mer-
gansers predict the maypole, leaping a few feet through the
air to dive in unison, the dolphins of duckdom. The wind
makes my eyes water.

Probably no one truly understands such a place. Certainly I don't. Except for wind and, more distantly today
than yesterday, the sound of the surf, it seems a quiet place
where nothing much is happening. Limbo. It awaits the migrants. Now we are between times.

Once there was no such thing as this marsh as I see it
now with its variety of vegetation, its wondrous tweedlike
texture of brown-through-tan grasses. That is because just
a few million years ago there were no grasses. They hadn't

evolved yet. God knows what marshlands looked like then. And now the marsh is being invaded, pushed out.

Today is a cool but sunny, gusty spring day. Tomorrow the forecast calls for the high sixties, a foretaste of summer. That's March for you. It can bring you winter one day, spring the next, then summer—in any order.

I wander the perimeters of the salt marsh not understanding much of what is certainly going on here and am reminded of the daddy of us all: Time. It shows up as moments—as when a frog ends its brief life in the long mandibles of a heron—or as an endless spiral. Leading where? Who knows?

To begin with, the marsh asks nothing of me. It is certainly no place now to get on with a desultory birder's life-list. But I confess that I am distracted and a bit worried about myrtle warblers, disorganized but all doing the same thing, hundreds of little yellow-rumped genetic programs looking for identical niches in this ultimately temporary marsh. What will their descendants do when the myrtle bushes ebb?

And what do I look for? Today, nothing more than the marsh, as unprepossessing as it is, with nothing much happening of an epochal nature. Just the marsh and me here today, and however trivial that may seem, in terms of my particular life-lists, it is enough.

FROM *Songs to Birds*

In the Pinewoods,
Crows and Owl

MARY OLIVER

Great bumble. Sleek
slicer. How the crows
dream of you, caught at last
in their black beaks. Dream of you
leaking your life away. Your wings
crumbling like old bark. Feathers
falling from your breast like leaves,
and your eyes two bolts
of lightning gone to sleep.
Eight of them
fly over the pinewoods looking down
into the branches. They know you are
there somewhere, fat and drowsy
from your night of rabbits and rats. Once
this month you caught a crow. Scraps of him
flew far and wide, the news

rang all day through the woods. The cold
river of their hatred roils
day and night: you are their dream, their waking,
their quarry, their demon. You
are the pine god who never speaks but holds
the keys to everything while they fly
morning after morning against the shut doors. You
will have a slow life, and eat them, one by one.
They know it. They hate you. Still
when one of them spies you out, all stream
straight toward violence and confrontation.
As though it helped to see the living proof.
The bone-crushing prince of dark days, gloomy
at the interruption of his rest. Hissing
and snapping, grabbing about him, dreadful
as death's drum; mournful, unalterable fact.

FROM *American Primitive*

The Passenger Pigeon

JOHN JAMES AUDUBON

If there is a tendency in our age to treat birds as numbers, rather than wild beings, there is a precedent for it, dating back to long before 1620, when the Pilgrims landed on Plymouth Rock. When Jacques Cartier sailed toward the islands in the Gulf of St. Lawrence, back in 1534, he saw gannets, murres, puffins, and kittiwakes, which were as "thick as a meadow with grass." His men landed on the cliffs and killed more than a thousand murre in a few hours, as well as great auks, flightless birds which were to become extinct as a result of their repeated slaughter by sailors arriving at the New World.

During the centuries of settlement, indiscriminate shooting of birds was commonplace. The abundance of the continent was feverishly admired, to the extent that killing off the wildlife seemed irresistible. Passenger pigeons, wild turkeys, prairie chickens, swallows, songbirds, shorebirds of all kinds, terns, egrets, swans, geese, ducks, "chicken hawks"—everything that was edible and much that was not—came close to extermination, before conservation laws were finally put into effect.

As Roy Bedichek, the Texas naturalist, put it in his book, Karankaway County, while describing the courtship of male prairie chickens in the spring, "contempt for wildlife on the frontier was almost beyond belief." There used to be killing contests in Texas which lasted for several days, the prize going to those who killed the most birds. Each contestant deposited the prairie chickens he had shot in a pile to be counted by the judges.

Bedichek continues, "It proved burdensome to have to bring in the whole bird, so sometimes contestants were permitted under the rules to be credited with heads only. Then the hunter shot his bird down, whacked off the head, stuffed it in a bag, and threw the body away."

Great piles of corpses lay rotting on the ground. These sporting events were repeated until the prairie chicken started to drop out of sight. A period of wholesale agriculture and development followed which destroyed its habitat. Today it is found only in small numbers.

Forbush describes a trip to the St. John's River in Florida, in the late 1790s: "Uncounted swarms of waterfowl of many species inhabited the waters in innumerable multitudes. Great flocks of White Egrets and Ibises, among them the lovely Roseate Spoonbills, possessed the land. Every turn in the river brought into view a new scene, to be scanned for novel forms of life."

To this he adds: "Practically all tourists were armed with rifles, shotguns, revolvers, or all three. These armed men lined the rails of the steamboats and shot ad libitum *at alligators, waterfowl, anything that made an attractive target. There were practically no restrictions on shooting, although the steamers never stopped to gather in the game, but left it to lie where it fell."*

After the great free-for-all of the frontier, we became increasingly disengaged from the land, perhaps as a result of our possession of it. As if we had never see it in the first place, we left its ancient identity behind us. We have even, it is said, left nature for dead. But birds remain, to teach us what they can of a universe which we have badly neglected.

The last passenger pigeon died in its cage at the Cincinnati Zoo in 1914. The demise of the passenger pigeon symbolizes this loss of wilderness.

⤳

Let us now, kind reader, inspect their place of nightly rendezvous. One of these curious roosting-places, on the banks of the Green River in Kentucky, I repeatedly visited. It was, as is always the case, in a portion of the forest where the trees were of great magnitude, and where there was little underwood. I rode through it upwards of forty miles, and, crossing it in different parts, found its average breadth to be rather more than three miles. My first view of it was about a fortnight subsequent to the period when they had made choice of it, and I arrived there nearly two hours before sunset. Few Pigeons were then to be seen, but a great number of persons, with horses and waggons, guns and ammunition, had already established encampments on the borders. Two farmers from the vicinity of Russelsville, distant more than a hundred miles, had driven upwards of three hundred hogs to be fattened on the pigeons which were to be

slaughtered. Here and there, the people employed in pluck-
ing and salting what had already been procured, were seen
sitting in the midst of large piles of these birds. The dung
lay several inches deep, covering the whole extent of the
roosting-place, like a bed of snow. Many trees two feet in
diameter, I observed, were broken off at no great distance
from the ground; and the branches of many of the largest
and tallest had given way, as if the forest had been swept
by a tornado. Every thing proved to me that the number of
birds resorting to this part of the forest must be immense
beyond conception. As the period of their arrival approached, their foes anxiously prepared to receive them.
Some were furnished with iron-pots containing sulphur,
others with torches of pine-knots, many with poles, and the
rest with guns. The sun was lost to our view, yet not a Pigeon had arrived. Every thing was ready, and all eyes were
gazing on the clear sky, which appeared in glimpses amidst
the tall trees. Suddenly there burst forth a general cry of
"Here they come!" The noise which they made, though yet
distant, reminded me of a hard gale at sea, passing through
the rigging of a close-reefed vessel. As the birds arrived and
passed over me, I felt a current of air that surprised me.
Thousands were soon knocked down by the pole-men. The
birds continued to pour in. The fires were lighted, and a
magnificent, as well as wonderful and almost terrifying,
sight presented itself. The Pigeons, arriving by thousands,
alighted everywhere, one above another, until solid masses
as large as hogsheads were formed on the branches all
round. Here and there the perches gave way under the
weight with a crash, and falling to the ground, destroyed
hundreds of the birds beneath, forcing down the dense
groups with which every stick was loaded. It was a scene of
uproar and confusion. I found it quite useless to speak, or

even to shout to those persons who were nearest to me. Even the reports of the guns were seldom heard, and I was made aware of the firing only by seeing the shooters reloading.

No one dared venture within the line of devastation. The hogs had been penned up in due time, the picking up of the dead and wounded being left for the next morning's employment. The Pigeons were constantly coming, and it was past midnight before I perceived a decrease in the number of those that arrived. The uproar continued the whole night: and as I was anxious to know to what distance the sound reached, I sent off a man, accustomed to perambulate the forest, who, returning two hours afterwards, informed me he had heard it distinctly when three miles distant from the spot. Towards the approach of the day, the noise in some measure subsided, long before objects were distinguishable, the Pigeons began to move off in a direction quite different from that in which they had arrived the evening before, and at sunrise all that were able to fly had disappeared. The howlings of the wolves now reached our ears, and the foxes, lynxes, cougars, bears, raccoons, oppossums and pole-cats were seen sneaking off, whilst eagles and hawks of different species, accompanied by a crowd of vultures, came to supplant them, and enjoy their share of the spoil.

It was then that the authors of all this devastation began their entry amongst the dead, the dying, and the mangled. The pigeons were picked up and piled in heaps, until each had as many as he could possibly dispose of, when the hogs were let loose to feed on the remainder.

FROM *Ornithological Biography:*
The Bird Biographies of John James Audubon

The Andean Condor

CHARLES DARWIN

Despite intense efforts to save it from extinction, the California condor is now reduced to some twenty individuals. Its decline can be attributed to the loss of its original range to extensive development, as well as to an indiscriminate use of pesticides. This magnificent bird, a biological and ecological treasure, has a wingspread of ten feet. Soaring through the air over the rugged mountain terrain where it lives, it can reach elevations of 15,000 feet.

The counterpart of the California variety is the Andean condor, once revered by the Incas, who engraved its image on rock walls, wove it into tapestries, and painted it on their pottery. Its range was the great spinal cord of the Andes along the western coast of South America. This species is still found in fair numbers, but it is steadily declining, owing in large part to hunters. Charles Darwin encountered the Andean condor during his five-year voyage on the Beagle, *from 1831 to 1836. He collected his observations in* The Voyage of the Beagle, *the precursor to his great work* On the Origin of Species, *published in 1859.*

⌁

APRIL 27TH: The bed of the river became rather narrower, and hence the stream more rapid. It here ran at the rate of six knots an hour. From this cause, and from the many great angular fragments, tracking the boats became both dangerous and laborious.

This day I shot a condor. It measured from tip to tip of the wings, eight and a half feet, and from beak to tail, four feet. This bird is known to have a wide geographical range, being found on the west coast of South America, from the Strait of Magellan, along the Cordillera as far as eight degrees N. of the equator. The steep cliff near the mouth of the Rio Negro is its northern limit on the Patagonian coast; and they have there wandered about four hundred miles from the great central line of their habitation in the Andes. Further south, among the bold precipices at the head of Port Desire, the condor is not uncommon; yet only a few stragglers occasionally visit the sea-coast. A line of cliff near the mouth of the Santa Cruz is frequented by these birds, and about eighty miles up the river, where the sides of the valley are formed by steep basaltic precipices, the condor reappears. From these facts it seems that the condors require perpendicular cliffs. In Chile, they haunt, during the greater part of the year, the lower country near the shores of the Pacific, and at night several roost together in one tree; but in the early part of summer, they retire to the most inaccessible parts of the inner Cordillera, there to breed in peace.

With respect to their propagation, I was told by the country people in Chile, that the condor makes no sort of nest, but in the months of November and December lays two large white eggs on a shelf of bare rock. It is said that the young condors cannot fly for an entire year; and long after they are able, they continue to roost by night, and hunt by day with their parents. The old birds generally live in pairs; but among the inland basaltic cliffs of the Santa Cruz, I found a spot, where scores must usually haunt. On coming suddenly to the brow of the precipice, it was a grand spectacle to see between twenty and thirty of these great birds start heavily from their resting-place, and wheel away in majestic circles. From the quantity of dung on the rocks, they must long have frequented this cliff for roosting and breeding. Having gorged themselves with carrion on the plains below, they retire to these favourite ledges to digest their food. From these facts, the condor, like the gallinazo, must to a certain degree be considered as a gregarious bird. In this part of the country they live altogether on the guanacos which have died a natural death, or, as more commonly happens, have been killed by the pumas. I believe, from what I saw in Patagonia, that they do not on ordinary occasions extend their daily excursions to any great distance from their regular sleeping-places.

The condors may oftentimes be seen at a great height, soaring over a certain spot in the most graceful circles. On some occasions I am sure that they do this only for pleasure, but on others, the Chileno countryman tells you that they are watching a dying animal, or the puma devouring its prey. If the condors glide down, and then suddenly all rise together, the Chileno knows that it is the puma which, watching the carcass, has sprung out to drive away the robbers. Besides feeding on carrion, the condors frequently attack young goats and lambs; and the shepherd dogs are trained, whenever they pass over, to run out, and looking upwards to bark violently. The Chilenos destroy and catch numbers. Two methods are used; one is to place a carcass on a level piece of ground within an enclosure of sticks with an opening, and when the condors are gorged to gallop up on horseback to the entrance, and thus enclose them: for when this bird has not space to run, it cannot give its body sufficient momentum to rise from the ground. The second method is to mark the trees in which, frequently to the number of five or six together, they roost, and then at night to climb up and noose them. They are such heavy sleepers, as I have myself witnessed, that this is not a difficult task. At Valparaiso, I have seen a living condor sold for sixpence, but the common price is eight or ten shillings. One which I saw brought in, had been tied with rope, and was much injured; yet, the moment the line was cut by which its bill was secured, although surrounded by people, it began ravenously to tear a piece of carrion. In a garden at the same place, between twenty and thirty were kept alive. They were fed only once a week, but they appeared in pretty good health. The Chileno countrymen assert that the condor will live, and retain its vigour, between five and six weeks without eating: I cannot answer for the truth of this, but it is a cruel experiment, which very likely has been tried.

When an animal is killed in the country, it is well known that the condors, like other carrion-vultures, soon gain intelligence of it, and congregate in an inexplicable manner. In most cases it must not be overlooked, that the birds have discovered their prey, and have picked the skeleton clean before the flesh is in the least degree tainted. Remembering the experiments of M. Audubon, on the little smelling powers of carrion-hawks, I tried in the above-mentioned garden the following experiment: the condors were tied, each by a rope, in a long row at the bottom of a wall; and having folded up a piece of meat in white paper, I walked backwards and forwards, carrying it in my hand at the distance of about three yards from them, but no notice whatever was taken. I then threw it on the ground, within one yard of an old male bird; he looked at it for a moment with attention, but then regarded it no more. With a stick I pushed it closer and closer, until at last he touched it with his beak; the paper was then instantly torn off with fury, and at the same moment, every bird in the long row began struggling and flapping its wings. Under the same circumstances, it would have been quite impossible to have deceived a dog. The evidence in favour of and against the acute smelling powers of carrion-vultures is singularly balanced. Professor Owen has demonstrated that the olfactory nerves of the turkey-buzzard (Cathartes aura) are highly developed; and on the evening when Mr. Owen's paper was read at the Zoological Society, it was mentioned by a gentleman that he had seen the carrion-hawks in the West Indies on two occasions collect on the roof of a house, when a corpse had become offensive from not having been buried: in this case the intelligence could hardly have been acquired by sight. On the other hand, besides the experiments of Audubon and that one by myself, Mr. Bachman has tried in the United States many varied plans, showing that neither the turkey-buzzard (the species dissected by Professor Owen) nor the gallinazo find their food by smell. He covered portions of highly offensive offal with a thin canvas cloth, and strewed pieces of meat on it; these the carrion-vultures ate up, and then remained quietly standing, with their beaks within the eighth of an inch of the putrid mass, without discovering it. A small rent was made in the canvas, and the offal was immediately discovered; the canvas was replaced by a fresh piece, and meat again put on it, and was again devoured by the vultures without their discovering the hidden mass on which they were trampling. These facts are attested by the signatures of six gentlemen, besides that of Mr. Bachman.

Often when lying down to rest on the open plains, on looking upwards, I have seen carrion-hawks sailing through the air at a great height. Where the country is level I do not believe a space of the heavens, of more than fifteen degrees above the horizon, is commonly viewed with any attention by a person either walking or on horseback. If such be the case, and the vulture is on the wing at a height of between three and four thousand feet, before it could come within the range of vision, its distance in a straight line from the beholder's eye, would be rather more than two British miles. Might it not thus readily be overlooked? When an animal is killed by the sportsman in a lonely valley, may he not all the while be watched from above by the sharp-sighted bird? And will not the manner of its descent proclaim throughout the district to the whole family of carrion-feeders, that their prey is at hand?

When the condors are wheeling in a flock round and round any spot, their flight is beautiful. Except when rising from the ground, I do not recollect ever having seen one of these birds flap its wings. Near Lima, I watched several for nearly half an hour, without once taking off my eyes: they moved in large curves, sweeping in circles, descending and ascending without giving a single flap. As they glided close over my head, I intently watched from an oblique position, the outlines of the separate and great terminal feathers of each wing, and these separate feathers, if there had been the least vibratory movement, would have appeared as if blended together; but they were seen distinct against the blue sky. The head and neck were moved frequently, and apparently with force; and the extended wings seemed to form the fulcrum on which the movements of the neck, body, and tail acted. If the bird wished to descend, the wings were for a moment collapsed; and when again expanded with an altered inclination, the momentum gained by the rapid descent seemed to urge the bird upwards with the even and steady movement of a paper kite. In the case of any bird *soaring,* its motion must be sufficiently rapid, so that the action of the inclined surface of its body on the atmosphere may counter-balance its gravity. The force to keep up the momentum of a body moving in a horizontal plane in the air (in which there is so little friction) cannot be great, and this force is all that is wanted. The movement of the neck and body of the condor, we must suppose, is sufficient for this. However this may be, it is truly wonderful and beautiful to see so great a bird, hour after hour, without any apparent exertion, wheeling and gliding over mountain and river.

FROM *The Voyage of the Beagle*

Wild Swans of the Chesapeake

GILBERT KLINGEL

The Bay, *from which the following was taken, was originally published in 1951. This was the period after World War II, when a new generation of writers, notably Rachel Carson, with her* The Sea around Us *and* The Edge of the Sea, *began to introduce a wide audience to the rich natural regions of the American continent.*

Gilbert Klingel complained that although much had been written about the waters of the tropics, little effort had been made to explore our own. He was not a practicing scientist, but The Bay *was the work of a naturalist on his home ground who explored the great Chesapeake region as a natural phenomenon. Aside from previous books that had concentrated on ships and seafarers, the romantic colonial past, and the estates along the*

*river banks, the Chesapeake had been curiously neglected. Klin-
gel wrote of barnacles, fiddler crabs, ospreys, herons, and fishes,
and the underwater worlds of many marvellous creatures, so as
to help right the balance.*

*Partly as a result of Klingel's work, forty-five years ago, the
"Save the Bay" movement began to try to overturn the drastic
changes that had polluted primal waters once wonderfully open
and productive. The famous blue crab is threatened with extinction, the striped bass has only recently been rescued, and
many other forms of life are sadly depleted, because of pollution
and the vast growth of population and industry.*

*The present state of affairs encourages conservation, but it is
even more important for us to look deeply into our native land
and its surrounding waters, so as to acquaint ourselves with the
irreplaceable life that must sustain us in the future.*

⤳

On a gray November day I saw on Eastern Bay in Maryland
what seemed a breath out of the fabled past. There was a
time within the memory of men when the skies over the
Bay were literally darkened by the passage of enormous
flocks of migrating birds, when across the firmament long
streamers of ducks, geese, and swans stretched for miles in
seemingly endless lines, passing at times for hours, when on
the feeding grounds the massed bodies of fowl obscured the
water for acres. The waterfowl still come but they come in
diminishing numbers; the sky-darkening flocks are a memory only and the living skeins of birds that once tapestried
the sky have degenerated into short, easily counted flights.
The years of constant slaughter have taken their toll and the
encroachments of a befouling civilization have muddied

the waters or poisoned the marshes and the flats until only a residue of the once-magnificent flocks remain to hint of what must have been.

But on this particular morning, in a gray dawn, I caught a glimpse of the glories of the days that have gone forever. All during the previous day a strong cold wind out of the northeast had been blowing, driving low clouds before it with occasional flurries of snow mixed with cold rain. But in the dark, and toward morning, the wind had shifted, moving to the southwest and bringing with it warm air and a dense penetrating fog.

And when the light came the fog hung low over the Bay hiding the buoys and the distant shore line and the mouths of the rivers. By then the wind had died and only the gentlest of ripples lapped against the sandy beaches. Because of the calm and the clinging damp of the fog it was very quiet, all except a faint murmuring which seemed to come out of the shrouded distance. At first I was not sure I heard it, but then it came again, clearer but still muted and indefinable.

My curiosity was stirred and I moved in its direction, toward the pine-clad tip of Kent Island, toward Bloody Point and the shallows that extend for long distances from that point and break the sea coming in from the open Chesapeake. Presently the sound became more distinct, an odd gabbling and a queer rustling and splashing. The noise appeared to cover a large arc of the invisible horizon and seemed to emanate from beyond the beach, out in the open water.

When I came close, when the individual sounds that made up the whole began to become distinguishable, the fog began to lift a little and there appeared not far from shore a white line as though foam was piled deep in billowy drifts. The line was so white against the gray that it seemed to give off a light of its own, a loom much like a reflection of snow. Then the fog lifted completely, and against a dark-green sea and a gray sky appeared one of the largest flocks of wild swan I have ever seen. There must have been nearly eight or nine hundred birds and they were massed together between the deep water and the beach.

Captivated by the unexpected display, for I never expected to see such a sight again, I circled inland over wet fields and through fog-dampened woods to approach the flock through a screen of dark-green pines and holly. By creeping through sheltering vines, from trunk to trunk, I managed to arrive undetected at the top of a small bluff overlooking the center of the gathering.

As I reached the edge and sank into the vegetation out of sight, a wonderful event occurred. At that very moment a rift must have opened somewhere in the clouds, for a long shaft of soft rose-colored light stole down through the overhanging mist and bathed the whole group in a luminescent glow. Against the somber background of gray sky and dull-green sea the sight of these hundreds of graceful, clean, curving bodies suddenly lighted with brilliant pink was exceedingly beautiful, and I rate it as one of the most enthralling spectacles I have ever witnessed. For a little while the matchless scene endured and then the color faded and the world was once again a monotone.

FROM *The Bay*

The Road Runner

JOSEPH WOOD KRUTCH

In The Voice of the Desert, *Joseph Wood Krutch wrote that this is the voice that has been least often heard. "We came to it last, and when we did come, we came principally to exploit and not to listen." What this scholarly and devoted naturalist did, after moving from the coast to Arizona, was to listen. He treated the animals and plants he met not just with a vague sympathy but with respect, as time-honored residents of an ancient neighborhood. He knew that he would never know very much about them, or the desert of which they were an essential part, unless he treated them with civility.*

To find an answer to the more interesting question; to find an animal which refuses to live anywhere *except* in the desert; to find one which is, in his own peculiar way, very demanding even though what he demands is what most animals would not have at any price, I do not have to go far. Indeed, I do not have to go any further from my doorstep than I went to find the spadefoot. And it happens that I intruded upon this perfect desert dweller at a dramatic moment only a few days ago when I stepped out in the early morning and was startled by a large chicken-sized bird— if you can still call him a bird—who was dashing madly back and forth at right angles to my line of vision. His headlong plunges were so like those of a frenzied hen who seems to be rushing madly in all directions at once, that for a moment I thought I had frightened him out of his wits. As it turned out, he was merely too busy at the moment to acknowledge my presence.

As to *what* he was, that question could be answered by even the most unobservant person who has ever driven a highway in the desert. He was one of the commonest, as well as perhaps the most remarkable, of all desert birds— namely a road runner—nearly two feet of relentless energy from the tip of his wicked bill to the tip of the long, expressive tail which may trail the ground when he is calm or depressed, or be raised almost as straight up as the tail of a confident cat when he is happily angry, as indeed he seems to be a good part of the time. From his bold bad eye to his springy tread everything proclaims him "rascal," and he has, in truth, a number of bad habits. But there is also something indescribably comic about him, and he illustrates the rule that comic rascals have a way of engaging the affection of even the virtuous. Nearly everybody is curiously cheered by the sight of a road runner. In the old days the cowboys used to be amused by his habit of racing ahead of their horses and they gave him his name. The Mexicans of Sonora call him affectionately "paisano" or "countryman."

My specimen, far from having lost his wits, had them

very much about him. Suddenly he arrested his mad career, stabbed with lightning rapidity at the ground and, crest erect, lifted his head triumphantly—with a good sized lizard in his beak. No one who has ever seen one of our lizards run would like to be assigned the task of chasing it from bush to bush and then nabbing it with a hand. But catching lizards is all in a day's work for a road runner and mine was merely collecting some for his breakfast. His diet is varied from time to time by a snake, or even an insect, if the insect happens to be large enough to be worth the effort of a leap from the ground to take him on the wing, as I have seen a zooming dragonfly taken. Responsible observers say that when the lizard tries his usual trick of surrendering his tail so that the rest of him may make a safe getaway, the road runner, unlike some other predators, is not to be fooled. He merely takes a firmer grip on the body and collects the discarded tail later. Scorpions are also quite acceptable as tidbits.

Inevitably such a creature is the center of many legends. There seems to be no doubt that he takes the killing of rattlesnakes in his stride, but old-timers insist that he sometimes first surrounds the snake with a circle of spiny cactus joints so that the snake cannot get away. In fact, only a few weeks ago a friend told me that one of *his* friends had seen a slight variation on this performance when a road runner walled the snake in with small stones before attacking him. But like the milk snake milking a cow and the hoop snake rolling merrily along with his tail in his mouth, this remarkable performance seems never to be witnessed by anyone with a professional interest in natural history and it is usually a friend of a friend who was on the spot. The situation seems much the same as that with ghosts. You are most likely to see them if you are a simple person and have faith.

As a matter of fact, however, you do not always have to be a simple or ignorant person to believe what the simple tell you. A well-educated man recently passed on to me the old superstition that the Gila monster, our only poisonous lizard, owed his venom to the unfortunate fact that nature had not provided him with any orifice through which the waste products of metabolism could be discharged, and that poisons therefore inevitably accumulated. One need only turn a Gila on his back to dispose of this legend which is sufficiently improbable on the face of it. Most of the people who repeat it have pointlessly taken part in the attempt to exterminate these creatures, but have obviously never looked at the bodies of their victims. And yet we still feel superior to the men of the Middle Ages who insisted that the toad had a precious jewel in his head, when they might so easily have found out that he didn't!

Of course it may just possibly turn out that the road runner really does fence his victims in. Stranger things do happen and the evidence against it is necessarily only negative. But the "paisano" is odd enough without the legends. Almost everything about him is unbird-like at the same time that it fits him to desert conditions. He is a bird who has learned how not to act like one.

Though he can fly—at least well enough to get to the top of a mesquite if there is some really urgent reason for doing so—he would rather not, trusting to his long legs to catch his prey and to get him out of trouble. The sound which he makes is like nothing on earth, least of all like a bird. One writer describes it as a sort of modified Bronx cheer, which is right enough since it seems to be made by the raucous expelling of air accompanied by a rapid gnashing of the bill—if a bill can be gnashed. Like the bird himself, the sound is derisive, irascible, ribald, threatening, and highly self-confident. As befits a no-nonsense sort of creature, the road runner is content to dress himself in neutral, brown-speckled feathers, but there is a line of red cuticle behind his eye which he can expose when it seems desirable to look a bit fiercer than usual.

Sociologists talk a great deal these days about "adjust-ment," which has always seemed to me a defeatist sort of word suggesting dismal surrender to the just tolerable. The road runner is not "adjusted" to his environment. He is tri-umphant in it. The desert is his home and he likes it. Other creatures, including many other birds, elude and compro-mise. They cling to the mountains or to the cottonwood-filled washes, especially in the hot weather, or they go away somewhere else, like the not entirely reconciled human in-habitants of this region. The road runner, on the other hand, stays here all the time and he prefers the areas where he is hottest and driest. The casual visitor is most likely to see him crossing a road or racing with a car. But one may see him also in the wildest wilds, either on the desert flats or high up in the desert canyons where he strides along over rocks and between shrubs. Indeed, one may see him almost anywhere below the level where desert gives way to pines or aspen.

He will come into your patio if you are discreet. Taken young from the nest, he will make a pet, and one writer describes a tame individual who for years roosted on top a wall clock in a living room, sleeping quietly through eve-ning parties unless a visitor chose to occupy the chair just below his perch, in which case he would wake up, descend upon the intruder, and drive him away. But the road runner

is not one who needs either the human inhabitant or anything which human beings have introduced. Not only his
food but everything else he wants is amply supplied in his
chosen environment. He usually builds his sketchy nest out
of twigs from the most abundant tree, the mesquite. He
places it frequently in a cholla, the wickedest of the cacti
upon whose murderous spines even snakes are sometimes
found fatally impaled. He feeds his young as he feeds himself, upon the reptiles which inhabit the same areas which
he does. And because they are juicy, neither he nor his
young are as dependent upon the hard-to-find water as the
seed-eating birds who must sometimes make long trips to
get it.

Yet all the road runner's peculiarities represent things
learned, and learned rather recently as a biologist understands "recent." He is not a creature who happened to have
certain characteristics and habits and who therefore survived here. This is a region he moved into and he was once
very different. As a matter of fact, so the ornithologists tell
us, he is actually a cuckoo, although no one would ever
guess it without studying his anatomy. Outwardly, there is
nothing to suggest the European cuckoo of reprehensible
domestic morals or, for that matter, the American cuckoo
or "rain crow" whose mournful note is familiar over almost
the entire United States and part of Canada—not exclud-
ing the wooded oases of Arizona itself. That cuckoo flies,
perches, sings and eats conventional bird food. He lives only
where conditions are suited to his habits. But one of his not
too distant relatives must have moved into the desert—
slowly, no doubt—and made himself so much at home
there that by now he is a cuckoo only to those who can read
the esoteric evidences of his anatomical structure.

Despite all this, it must be confessed that not everybody

loves the road runner. Nothing is so likely to make an animal unpopular as a tendency to eat things which we ourselves would like to eat. And the road runner is guilty of just this wickedness. He is accused, no doubt justly, of varying his diet with an occasional egg of the Gambel's quail, or even with an occasional baby quail itself. Sportsmen are afraid that this reduces somewhat the number they will be able to kill in their own more efficient way and so, naturally, they feel that the road runner should be eliminated.

To others it seems that a creature who so triumphantly demonstrates how to live in the desert ought to be regarded with sympathetic interest by those who are trying to do the same thing. He and the quail have got along together for quite a long time. Neither seems likely to eliminate the other. Man, on the other hand, may very easily eliminate both. It is the kind of thing he is best at.

FROM *The Voice of the Desert*

Spring in the
Arctic Wilderness

KNUD RASMUSSEN

Knud Rasmussen was born in Jacobshavn, Greenland, in 1879, the son of a Danish father and an Eskimo mother. He died in 1933. Rasmussen was trained in ethnology and anthropology in Copenhagen, Denmark, and undertook a number of expeditions in his native Greenland to study and record the customs, folklore, songs, and stories of the native people, in the face of advancing Western culture. He was also a highly courageous and skilled explorer. Between 1921 and 1924, he crossed the continent by dog sled, all the way from Greenland to the Bering Strait.

☙

On land, one heard all around the little singing sound of melting snow; and the daylight beat so fiercely on the whiteness of the lake that one had to shade one's eyes. Spring had come to the Barren Grounds, and soon earth and flowers would rearise out of the snow.

Small herds of caribou on the move approached within easy distance; but today we were friendly observers only, and felt nothing of the hunter's quickened pulse on seeing them at close range. We had meat enough for the present.

Here again we found the stone barriers, shelters and clumsy figures built to represent a human form, with a lump of peat for a head—relics of the days when caribou hunting was carried on systematically by driving the animals down to the water, where the kayak men were ready to fall upon them with the spear.

With the introduction of firearms, this method of hunting has gone out of fashion, and there will soon be hardly a kayak left in the Barren Grounds. But not many years ago, these inland people were as bold and skilful in the management of a kayak as any of the natives on the coast.

Igjugarjuk and I walked down towards the camp. Far out on the horizon one could see the extreme fringe of the forest, but the sunlight was deceptive, and I could hardly make out for certain whether it were trees or hill. I asked Igjugarjuk, and he answered at once: "Napartut" (the ones that stand up). "Not the true forest where we fetch wood for our long sledges; that is farther still. It is our belief that the trees in a forest are living beings, only that they cannot speak; and for that reason we are loth to spend the night among them. And those who have at some time had to do so, say that at night, one can hear a whispering and groaning among the trees, in a language beyond our understanding.". . .

But by the open waters of the lake there was an incessant chattering among the gulls and terns and duck who cannot make out why the loon should always utter such a mournful cry in its happiest moments. There was a blessedness of life and growth here in the spring, when the long-frozen earth at last breathed warm and soft and moist, and plants could stretch their roots in the soil and their branches above. The sand by the river bank gleamed white; showing clearly the footprints of the cranes as they moved. All the birds were talking at once, heedless of what was going on around them, until a flock of wild geese came swooping down, raising a mighty commotion in the water as they alighted. And in face of these, the smaller fry were silent and abashed. But who can paint the sounds of spring? The nature lover will not attempt it, but will be content to breathe its fragrance with rejoicing.

The sun was low on the horizon, the sky and the land all around aglow with flaming color.

"A youth is dead and gone up into the sky," said Igjugarjuk. "And the Great Spirit colors earth and sky with a joyful red to receive his soul."

FROM *Across Arctic America*

Part Five

Birds of the Sea

Most seabirds are roamers, at home in the wide and various ranges of the oceans of the world. Except when returning to land during the nesting season, they forage for food over great distances. Their displays, during the times when we can observe them, are elaborate. Their manner of flight varies from auks and penguins, which seem to fly underwater, to the racy, soaring frigate birds, with their dynamic maneuverability. A colony of gannets atop a high cliff or a flock of terns on sandy islands produces gutteral, shrill sounds not unlike the clamor of our own cities. The British naturalist Edward Armstrong wrote,

> there is a vitalizing thrill in being amongst a multitudinous host of creatures; when these are big, elegant and powerful birds in the full vigour of breeding activities the experience is almost akin to exaltation. The gannets sweep around the stark cliffs, riding gracefully on the wind, alighting with flapping wings and depressed tail to stand ponderously on the rocks; then launching forth again with a hoarse *rraah* and sudden downward plunge. In the distance the birds look like a flurry of giant snowflakes, but when we reach

the summit of the precipice and look over we see that the
ledges right down to the surf-swept rocks are crowded with
gannets, for the most part adults, guarding a nestling, or
incubating; but here and there are immature birds, in their
first, second and third year, recognisable by their dark,
flecked plumage. (*Bird Display and Behavior,* 1947; reprint,
New York: Dover Publications, 1964)

The Seafarer

ANONYMOUS

*This famous Anglo Saxon poem was composed between A.D. 650
and 1000, before the Norman Conquest. At first reading, it may
seem only to reflect the suffering of a sailor, but note the profound way he is drawn to the sea. He joins with the gannets,
the terns, wanderers over the stretch of the seas. He is as familiar
with the cry of a curlew as with the calling of the gulls.*

I can utter a true song about myself, tell of my travels, how
in toilsome days I often suffered a time of hardship, how I
have borne bitter sorrow in my breast, made trial of many
sorrowful abodes on ships; dread was the rolling of the
waves. There the hard night-watch at the boat's prow was
often my task, when it tosses by the cliffs. Afflicted with
cold, my feet were fettered by frost, by chill bonds. There
my sorrows, hot round my heart, were sighed forth; hunger

within rent the mind of the sea-weary man. The man who
fares most prosperously on land knows not how I, care-
worn, have spent a winter as an exile on the ice-cold sea, cut
off from kinsmen, hung round with icicles. The hail flew
in showers. I heard naught there save the sea booming, the
ice-cold billow, at times the song of the swan. I took my
gladness in the cry of the gannet and the sound of the curlew instead of the laughter of men, in the screaming gull
instead of the drink of mead. There storms beat upon the
rocky cliffs; there the tern with icy feathers answered them;
full often the dewy-winged eagle screamed around. No pro-
tector could comfort the heart in its need. And yet he who
has the bliss of life, who, proud and flushed with wine, suf-
fers few hardships in the city, little believes how I often in
weariness had to dwell on the ocean-path. The shadow of
night grew dark, snow came from the north, frost bound
the earth; hail fell on the ground, coldest of grain. And yet
the thoughts of my heart are now stirred that I myself
should make trial of the high streams, of the tossing of the
salt waves; the desire of the heart always exhorts to venture
forth that I may visit the land of strange people far hence.
And yet there is no man on earth so proud, nor so generous
of his gifts, nor so bold in youth, nor so daring in his deeds,
nor with a lord so gracious unto him, that he has not always
anxiety about his seafaring, as to what the Lord will bestow
on him. His thoughts are not of the harp, nor of receiving
rings, nor of delight in a woman, nor of joy in the world,
nor of aught else save the rolling of the waves; but he who
sets out on the waters ever feels longing. The groves put
forth blossoms; cities grow beautiful; the fields are fair; the
world revives; all these urge the heart of the eager-minded
man to a journey, him who thus purposes to fare far on the
ways of the flood. Likewise the cuckoo exhorts with sad

voice; the harbinger of summer sings, bodes bitter sorrow to the heart. The man knows not, the prosperous being, what some of those endure who most widely pace the paths of exile. And yet my heart is now restless in my breast, my mind is with the sea-flood over the whale's domain; it fares widely over the face of the earth, comes again to me eager and unsatisfied; the lone-flier screams, resistlessly urges the heart to the whale-way over the stretch of seas.

Wherefore the joys of the Lord are more inspiring for me than this dead fleeting life on earth. I have no faith that earthly riches will abide for ever. Each one of three things is ever uncertain ere its time comes; illness or age or hostility will take life away from a man doomed and dying. Wherefore the praise of living men who shall speak after he is gone, the best of fame after death for every man, is that he should strive ere he must depart, work on earth with bold deeds against the malice of fiends, against the devil, so that the children of men may later exalt him and his praise live afterwards among the angels for ever and ever, the joy of life eternal, delight amid angels.

FROM *Anglo Saxon Poetry*

The Quest for Survival

FRANKLIN RUSSELL

Seabirds are a wonderfully resourceful and varied race. Their adaptation to the environment impresses you less than their co-existence with it, their inclusion in the vast, ever-turning medium of the world ocean. Many of them are still only partly known to biologists, because for much of the year they are beyond sight or study. They belong to a distant frontier. Clearly, however, they are tough survivors; they have to be, as Franklin Russell emphasizes in the following passages from his book The Sea Has Wings.

⌁

As I watch seabirds coming in to land, I am reminded less of the millions of new lives about to be created than I am of the struggle that has taken place to reach these breeding havens. At least the island is a shelter. The sea is not. To survive and reach the island at all, the seabird must be master of his plastic, hostile, contrary world.

It is common during storms to see petrels darting along the troughs of waves, pausing every now and then to feed. There, they may be joined by rapidly flying murres who also use the lea of the wave for protection. Standing in my fragile boat which rises and falls in the great waves, I can admire this trick because I am leaning dangerously into the awesome power of the wind. Occasionally, I have seen such birds unwisely rise to the crests of spuming waves, only to be whipped away in a second in the grip of the wind.

Sometimes, far out to sea in a fishing boat, I have heard the crash of bodies hitting the superstructure, or the twang of stays and radio wires as helpless birds smashed into them. Once, when I was sitting in the warmth of the main cabin of a large fishing boat, a pair of murres struck the cabin door with such impact that they burst its flimsy catch and landed sprawling on our supper table. The blow would have killed ordinary birds but the murres kicked all the dishes off the table, bounced from wall to ceiling and dived under bunks before we could catch them and throw them back into the strength of the storm. It was an odd feeling, knowing they were more at home out there than in the relative calm of our cabin.

The sea offers no sinecures. Occasionally, a gale may abruptly change its direction ninety degrees. The waves, of course, are still possessed by the impetus of hundreds of miles of buildup and they cannot change direction. Now, the wind is sweeping along the troughs. There is no shelter, and the wind funnels along the troughs. Petrels, murres, and many other kinds of seabirds are swept away. If there is a mass of land in the path of the wind, they will be driven ashore. Then there will be what ornithologists descriptively call a "wreck."

These wrecks reveal a tiny part of the inner life of the seabird. A wreck occurs when all the resources of the sea-bird have become exhausted and he is a pure victim of the sea. I remember once being out on the ice pack in the Gulf of St. Lawrence during a spring blizzard which had gath-ered thousands of seabirds from the open water along the shores of southern Newfoundland and had pushed them into an unbroken world of ice. The birds, dovekies and murres, were in a doubly hostile environment, without shel-ter, where any attempt to land meant the high risk of mortal injury or crippling.

Some murres, desperately trying to fly diagonally against the wind and snow, lost control. They crashed into the ice and cartwheeled like spinning marionettes. Others chose to fly with the wind, but their strength exhausted, they crashed into upended ice floes and were killed. I found small groups of murres and dovekies huddled together in pathetic groups in the lea of ice hummocks, birds so beaten that I could pick them up. They lay in my hands without struggling.

It is easy to imagine seabird disasters in winter, but the sea is impartial and hands out disaster any month in the year. Summer storms, although rare, usually strike with shocking suddenness. They drive offshore fishing birds hundreds of miles from their islands, or kill them against the shores of their own breeding places. Almost the entire maritime region we are watching is the focus of two op-posing weather systems which create a great meteorological meat grinder which may stretch from Greenland to the Gulf of St. Lawrence. It is composed of a southern system rotating counterclockwise, colliding with a northern system rotating clockwise. The meshing gears of the two systems can ram gales due west across the maritime region and thence, inland.

These gales have great force and may blow uninterruptedly for days. Seabirds riding out such a storm well offshore are tested to see if their strength can match that of the meat grinder. If they weaken before the storm does, they are forced to ride with it, creating the ingredients of a wreck. Once, thousands of murres wintering in the Gulf of St. Lawrence and elsewhere found themselves caught in such a meat grinder and were swept west into the narrowing funnel of the St. Lawrence river estuary. They lacked sea room in which to maneuver and had long since lost the strength to fly against the wind. They were driven quickly over land where, disoriented even more, they were smashed all along a westward course stretching to Montreal and up the St. Lawrence to Toronto and into the Great Lakes region. Some of these birds, which I must assume were more panic-stricken than exhausted, even reached Indiana.

I have no doubt that in such wrecks psychology is involved. The murres are wrecked, but the puffins are not. While the puffins are stoically riding out the storm on the surface of the waters, the murres are in panicky flight and being swept away overhead. The reason for this difference in behavior, I like to assume, is the same reason that sends the murres joyously aloft at mating time while the puffins stay soberly and silently afloat.

Two birdmen, Peter Freuchen and Finn Salomonsen, once noticed that thousands of murres in west Greenland became panicky in December and January when the fiords of the island froze and they could not find open water. Here, the psychology of panic became strong. "They keep flying around in flocks searching for open water," the two men wrote. "And then eventually fall down on the ice, exhausted or stricken with panic at not being able to find water. Sometimes they stray over the land, where they soon succumb and are found dead or dying, often far from the sea."

The adaptation of seabirds to their world is ingenious enough, but like that of all other animals it tends to be inflexible. Any sudden variation in the norm is difficult for the creatures to accept. Sometimes the meat grinder may last long enough to sweep birds from the coasts of Greenland and throw its victims ashore all along the maritime strand.

A Quebec hunter of the nineteenth century, Napoléon Comeau, once saw dovekies passing his northern gulf coastline for two weeks, almost without a break, millions of them heading west. Here, too, was the suggestion of panic. The birds had been panicked by some earlier, distant storm that Comeau himself had not witnessed. But once the wreck was begun, there was nothing that could stop it.

Perhaps the worst bird wreck in history involved dovekies and it took a bizarre and unexpected direction. Through some unrecorded conjunction of events, the overwintering dovekies of the Greenland area found themselves caught in a meat grinder type of disaster, but one which spun them off southwest rather than due west. They found themselves driven far south along the Atlantic shore, moving parallel to it for thousands of miles, but as their resistance and will collapsed, they were driven inshore almost along the full length of the coastline.

They came inshore as mute and bizarre victims in totally alien places. Most of these small auks had never seen men or their works. They dropped down into small New England ponds set in the woods, and were unable to take off because of the surrounding trees. They starved to death. They flew into the doors of open freight cars in New York; the doors were shut and the dovekies were dispatched to certain deaths in the Middle West. They came sweeping into the Carolinas, carried by the universally high winds of the storm, and died in their uncounted hundreds when they crashed into electric light and telephone lines. They were found dead by the hundreds along the beaches of Florida, and some of them, presumably in the same kind of panic that sent murres to Indiana, fetched up along the shores of Cuba.

Only a very few of the seabirds' disasters are seen by men, but we do know that they are not critical to their survival as species. Almost all of them are long-lived, a testimony to their toughness and mastery of their world through their special skills.

All of the auks have the supreme capacity to swim and hunt fish underwater, a skill they have gained at the cost of strong flight. This is a sensible evolution since they swim all the time and fight wind storms only occasionally. Less sensible, however, is the apparent stupefaction of dovekies by cold, even though they are northern birds. When the temperature drops low enough in the waters of the Labrador current, they huddle together in small, pathetic rafts of creatures where, like the birds seeking refuge on the ice pack, they may be picked up unresisting from the water by passing fishermen.

Despite these odd anomalies, it remains the toughness of the seabirds that scores the memory. The greater shearwater breeds mainly on Tristan da Cunha, an island in the central section of the South Atlantic, midway between Africa and South America. Between nesting seasons, the greater shearwaters spend about eight months at sea without sighting

land. They crisscross the great ocean in flights that may total one hundred thousand miles or more in a year while
traveling from about thirty-seven degrees south latitude to
sixty degrees north latitude and back. The Arctic tern
flights, practically from pole to pole, are even more impressive. But all seabirds cover vast distances in conditions
that make it difficult for us to understand how they navigate, how they can so accurately pinpoint remote islands,
survive the gales, the cold, the ice.

Survival, for the seabird, depends on being in perfect
physical condition. It may be my imagination, but it has always seemed that seabirds *feel* different when handled.
Their bodies are more compact, more tightly muscled than
landbirds, and their strength is surprising, if they choose to
struggle. The first time I picked up a shearwater, caught in
a fisherman's hook on the Grand Banks, I thought the long-
winged, small-bodied bird would be easy to hold while we
got the hook out of his throat. But to my surprise, his body
was like a steel ball, his paddle feet, armed with sharp claws,
so badly flailed and slashed my hands that I almost dropped
him. Before we got control of him, he had ripped a piece
of flesh clean out of my hand. And all this damage was
done by a bird that looked about as dangerous as a pigeon.
Anyone who has picked up a puffin can testify to the effec-
tiveness of the vicelike bite from that heavy beak.

The murre himself is so physically tough that I have seen
fishermen put three and four barrels of birdshot into passing birds, and watched feathers and blood gouts bursting
from their bodies without causing them to swerve from
their flight. A Canadian ornithologist, Leslie Tuck, once
watched a murre and a peregrine falcon in a furious fight
on the slopes of Akpatok Island, in the sub-Arctic. Murre
and falcon tumbled down a scree slope, the falcon clenching

the murre with both talons. But at the bottom of the slope, the murre struggled so furiously that the falcon eventually let go and flew off. The murre, badly injured, staggered to his feet, and with great difficulty, got into the air himself.

This physical toughness is complemented by the seabirds' feathers. Their feathers are denser and more compact than those of landbirds. This sheath of feathers is, of course, the sole barrier between the seabird and death. A dramatic example of deficient feathering is the cormorant. He has made only a partial adaptation so far to the rigors of marine life. He can be seen in clumsy stances on the shore, with his wings bent away from his body as he tries to dry the plumage as quickly as possible. With his plumage wet, he would sink or be unable to take off, and then would drown.

The care and attention of the feather, therefore, is one of the first duties of the seabird. I have watched herring gulls standing in serried ranks on sand banks spending wholesale hours working their preening beaks from one end of their bodies to the other, flattening, arranging, pulling, and smoothing the feather cover.

One of the prime functions of preening is to spread the secretion of fatty material from the gland in the bird's tail all over the feathers in order to get a waterproof sheath. The oil not only waterproofs but also helps to keep the vane-like structure of each feather securely placed in its correct position. The seabird feather, like all feathers, is interconnected by a series of barbs that keeps each unit locked together in an almost impenetrable, propellerlike vane which enables both flying and swimming.

But the feathers do not perform this function automatically, and it is my impression that as the seabird grows older, he must spend longer each day at work on his plumage if he wants to survive. I once knew an old gull who could have been a score or more years old and he never spent less than two hours every morning preening himself on an old wharf piling post. To see him nibbling and poking, gently chewing and drawing feathers through his beak, helped to give me some insight into the realities of his life; he was the fighter preparing himself for the battle of the day that lay ahead.

Survival at sea is based on many imponderables. No creature could possibly guard against all of them. Birds are like human fliers, bound on apparently routine flights, who are led astray by wind, or fog, into faulty navigation that takes them to destruction. Seabirds avoid most of the traps set for them by the sea, but shorebirds or landbirds sometimes give us a dramatic example of the scope of oceanic treachery. In the thirties, a flight of lapwings from central England set out to migrate to Ireland. But their destination was covered by fog and so they overflew it and plunged out into the open Atlantic. Lapwings cannot settle on water, so their flight, to be successful, had to be uninterrupted. Thousands of them made this incredible journey and fetched up against the shores of Greenland, Labrador, Newfoundland, and Nova Scotia. The causes of that disaster remain enigmatic, but its quality, its all-embracing involvement, is the truth of the marine world.

Let us take another instance. It is June, the place Bonaventure Island. In the middle of a great fog with a strong east wind blowing, about twenty jaegers land on the island or circle it. These are birds who have come as much as two thousand miles from their Arctic hunting grounds. Their appearance at Bonaventure indicates some northern disaster.

Or, in the same place, an April snow storm blankets the island and suddenly five thousand fox sparrows are seen

from one end of the island to the other scratching in the
snow in search of food. The reality of the seabirds' world
grips the landbird as well. The mortalities of those attempting to make cross-sea migrations are also a commentary on
the lives of the seabirds.

All remains unpredictable, unexpected. Fulmars appear
abruptly in the southern Gulf of St. Lawrence. They come
out of the mists, circle my boat, and then disappear back
into the mist without offering any clue as to why they
should be so many thousands of miles from their hunting
grounds. Then, days later, I see glaucous gulls stalking the
rocks of Bonaventure Island or Bird Rock in the middle of
the Gulf, or flying along St. John's Harbor in Newfoundland, and wonder again why these Arctic creatures have
come south in the middle of summer when they should be
breeding in the north.

There is one certain truth about this world and that is its
total uncertainty. No uniformity of winter, no common de-
nomination of storm, no agreement about the duration of
sunshine or the length of mists obscuring thousands of
square miles of shore and sea alike.

Catastrophe comes out of a pure blue sky or out of a star-
studded night as easily as it does from the guts of a howling
gale. Once, at the height of the breeding season, a prema-
ture hurricane struck into this coastal world. The sea wind
was so strong that at Bonaventure not even the powerful
gannets could cope with it. Those birds nesting on the tops
of the cliffs were luckiest; with the great gusts, magnified
to eighty miles an hour by the wind shooting up the cliff
faces, they could overfly their nests without colliding with
the cliffs. Some of them, however, were already so low in
flight that they were swept among stunted spruce growth

hundreds of feet back from the cliff top and were impaled, like the victims of a human-type massacre, on the sharp spikes of the spruce branches.

For those birds making their landfall against the sheer walls of the cliffs, their landings had to be absolutely accurate. All that day of the storm, during which time the wind did not diminish, dozens of birds died. They came to the castle walls of the cliffs and smashed into bare rock. Or, just as unlucky, they collided in midair with others while straining to master the turbulence of wind rushing upward. Or they were caught in one-hundred-mile-an-hour gusts which sent them spinning into crevices where they were smashed.

As the winds continued, the waves heightened. Soon, one of these waves, perhaps a legendary "ninth wave," struck up the vertical cliff face more than fifty feet. The wave lifted thousands of tons of water upward and scoured the cliff face like some liquid cleaner. It reached the lower levels of nesting gannets and everything was swept away—adults, eggs, chicks—leaving the cliff bare and dripping.

Within an hour, another ninth wave, but this one much bigger, hurled a solid body of water almost to the tops of the cliffs. The rise of the water was majestic and massive. Thousands of adult gannets could see disaster looming and flung themselves away from the cliffs. Some were lucky and escaped, but other were caught as the wave peaked out, exploded at its crest, and roared backward, breaking inside itself and carrying hundreds of birds down with it.

At dawn of the following morning, with the wind subsided but the sea remaining a white torrent at the foot of the cliffs, the tide receded and revealed hundreds of injured, dying, and dead gannets. One night of the seabird was over.

Catastrophes are not always so dramatic. Days of prolonged rain and cold winds are more subtle disasters. Young herring gulls, only recently hatched, are vulnerable, as are young terns. With the rains falling day after day, the efforts of parents to shield the young from the downfall and the wind become a pathetic study in failure. Quite suddenly, just as the murres become undone, the resistance of the gulls or terns breaks down, and the chicks begin dying. In a really bad mortality, a kind of static wreck this, tens of thousands of youngsters may die.

No less dangerous may be a sharp gale occurring within weeks of the young gulls first achieving independence from their parents. Then, just beginning to acquire confidence in flight, but not realizing how truly callow are their wings, they fall victim to collisions with wave tops, trees, the rigging of vessels, and all kinds of other obstructions. Then, they may be seen in groups, walking up and down the beaches and rocks of the shores, their broken wings dangling uselessly.

The new day dawns and the gray seas tumble white as far as the eye can see. Five hundred miles from shore the black shapes of seabirds speed across the roiling waves. They have survived the night, the snow, predatory fish, the falcons and the eagles, the icing of their feathers, and they have come through to live another day. But they mock our own notions of security and question the real meaning of survival on this earth.

FROM *The Sea Has Wings*

Sea-Going of the Murre Chicks

LESLIE M. TUCK

Leslie Tuck, a Canadian biologist, follows the first, perilous journey of murre chicks from their nesting cliffs out onto the open sea. Mortality among young birds is normally quite high, even in the best years. In arctic or subarctic regions where fledgling auks, geese, ducks, or other species may have to fall from a cliff when leaving their nests in order to reach parents or safer habitats, the risk is particularly high. It is a tribute to their hardy natures that a majority usually survives. They have evolved, however, alongside great extremes of weather and seas. They exist within the context of lasting exposure to what both protects and endangers them.

———

Chicks sometimes take to the sea before they are sufficiently homoiothermic. In the excitement of sea-going, the cliffs are sometimes nearly deserted by the adults, and many chicks too young to survive life in the sea jump off the cliffs to the milling adults below or follow the adults and large chicks into the sea. Some of those helpless young birds are soon picked off by gulls. Some drown and others succeed in reaching land again, where, huddled on rocks and low ledges, they perish during the night. A chick fully thermo-regulated and with feathers resistant to the water, rides high. A chick not so well developed gets water-soaked and sinks lower and lower in the water. Deaths from this cause may on some days be as high as 10 per cent of the young birds going to sea. They probably become progressively less numerous, since the excitement of sea-going is highest during its first three or four days.

If the land-coming of murres is exciting, the sea-going is even more so. For a few days before the chicks are ready to go to sea, adults congregate at the base of the cliffs and call excitedly. There are no joy-flights and water-dances such as characterized the land-coming, but the formation of a milling congestion of birds in which numbers and noise are outstanding is a feature of murres' behaviour at this time. At first such groups concentrate a little way off shore. As time goes by, the groups become larger and the birds spend more time close inshore, at the very base of the cliffs. At a densely occupied colony, thousands of adults in a compact mass gather at the base of the cliffs, calling excitedly, when the sea-going period arrives. Such early groups are probably nonbreeders or birds which have lost their eggs or young, but at the critical time of sea-going they are joined by increasing numbers of breeding birds.

At Funk Island on some calm evening during the middle

of July—the date of first sea-going varied by only four days during three years of observation there—adults and grown chicks walk to the sea over the low smooth rock. They have particular routes, which are used annually, each leading towards a low part of the island where the sea washes ashore. Each of the three separate nesting groups has two or more such traditional paths to the sea. Several of the routes are nearly direct, but others, because of faults in the rock or other obstacles, are long and winding.

For several days before the first sea-going, adults congregate close inshore at evening and call excitedly. An even more noticeable change takes place within the nesting colonies. A large number of adults spread out loosely from the colonies, so that they now occupy a much greater area. The nesting colonies appear to be expanding and spilling over into the sea. Adults gather at the edge of the water. If flying birds alight on the island, they do so more frequently on the borders of the colonies than in their midst.

At that stage many of the chicks, especially the large ones, wander out towards the fringes of the colonies. Some of the adults and chicks then begin a slow procession towards the sea. The gross appearance of the colony changes again as the loitering birds on the fringes either join the procession or rush towards the sea to call anxiously. The birds at the head of the procession may hesitate for a short time on reaching the sea, but more frequently they plunge directly into the water or permit a wave to wash them off. They join the excited throng a few feet off shore.

There appears to be no competition between the adults of Funk Island for possession of chicks at sea. Just before darkness sets in, the processions towards the sea have ceased. More and more single adults leave the inshore concentration and return to the island. The remaining adults and chicks now move farther out to sea. Here and there can be seen a single adult and chick, separated from the others. They work farther and farther out to sea. By early morning they are scattered, each chick with a single adult, several miles from the island. Very rarely do two adults accompany a chick to sea at Funk Island, and if so, there is no evidence that both adults remain with the chick.

Each evening thereafter, unless it is stormy, adults and chicks wend their way towards the sea and the same sequence of events occurs. At Funk Island, the greatest number of birds leaves the island on the third or fourth day of sea-going. After that, for several weeks, smaller numbers leave each evening. Eventually the island is deserted.

Numerous chicks not fully developed and too young to survive away from land, join in the sea-going. They come from the fringes of the nesting colony, which is mostly deserted by adults at that time. Some of those young birds follow the others into the water. Most of them quickly become water-soaked and drown. Those which reach shore again invariably die from exposure on their way back to the colony.

Some of the very young birds at the edge of the sea are surrounded by adults, seemingly to prevent their entering the water, and just before dark they follow the adults back to the nesting colonies. On their way back to the colony many of those very young ones cannot overcome the obstacles they surmounted on their way downward. They perish during the night. In spite of such losses, adult protection at the sea edge may very well save a large number of the chicks which tend to go to sea prematurely. Nørrevang noted similar behaviour by the cliff-nesting common murres in the Faeroes. He wrote: "Also other young on the ledge showed unease, but the parent birds seemed to prevent them from coming to the edge by standing on the edge with the back turned to the sea, a most unusual position, the birds normally standing breast to the sea."

The sea-going of common murre chicks from cliffs is different from that described for Funk Island, where they literally walk off into the water. At the time of the sea-going of both species, the chicks' primaries are not yet developed, but they must make their plunge into the sea, sometimes from great heights. Kay describes the sea-going of common murre chicks from the cliffs in Shetland:

"On July 31, 1946, at the famous bird-cliffs at Noss, in the Shetland Islands . . . birds started coming off the cliffs at 8 p.m., the peak was at 10 p.m. and the flight lasted for another hour . . . The large majority of these young birds flew down each accompanied by one parent, the youngster flying from three to six feet in advance of, or to the side of the adult. Both alighted on the water . . . then immediately rushed towards each other, the parent calling loudly and excitedly, evidently fully aware of the danger in separation. Both birds now swam leisurely towards the open sea, the young bird very close to its parent's side. A few of the young ones were accompanied on their flight by two adults, presumably both parents . . . A number came down alone . . ."

Nørrevang describes a similar flight of common murre chicks at the Faeroe Islands. Several times he watched the actual flight from the ledges and remarked that one of the parents followed the chick as it leapt from the ledge. Nørrevang also noted that the young were never seen to leave the ledge alone.

The sea-going of thick-billed murre chicks differs from that of common murre chicks mainly in frequent competition between the adults for possession of a chick.

I have seen thick-billed murre chicks leaving the breeding cliffs at three large colonies. The most impressive was at Akpatok Island, where the ledges were some 500 feet above our camp and the chicks had to make a half-mile "flight" to reach the sea.

The first sea-going on Akpatok Island in 1955 occurred at dusk on the evening of August 26. At the start of sea-going, as many as seven adults accompanied a single chick on its outward flight, the chick calling shrilly, first plunging downward, then levelling out somewhat, beating its wings furiously. Invariably, one adult would be close to the chick, the others spread out in V-formation close behind. Frequently the adults used a beautiful, slow, butterfly-like flight, during which their wings arched over their backs, nearly touching. The group splashed into the water close together. Immediately other adults already in the water, or those flying around, closed in and all surrounded the chick. The chick was jostled, apparently pecked at and "hounded" continuously. It frequently dived, and then most or all of the adults dived simultaneously. Occasionally, all the adults took flight, leaving the chick alone for a time. Soon the same adults or others returned. Eventually all but a few lost interest or moved off to join the party surrounding another newly-arrived chick. Finally, a single adult remained with the chick and both went out to sea.

As the sea-going continued, the last chicks leaving the ledges were accompanied by single adults or even made the flight alone. Most of the adults were now concentrated in the water.

During the next few days chicks were taken as far as 20 miles to sea for experimental purposes and released. Always they were joined by a group of adults and the same sequence of mobbing and eventual leading away by a single adult took place. Sometimes we released a chick when there was no adult nearby. It was amazing how quickly adults flying some distance away were attracted by the shrill cries of the chick in the water and gathered around it.

Fisher and Lockley described this mobbing of chicks in the water: "The arrival of the chick upon the water excites the whole group of adults in the immediate vicinity . . . They surround it when it comes to the surface, and they may even make mock attacks, forcing it to submerge for a moment . . . The incident ends in the youngster swimming close to the adult which most persistently answers its calls, and it is led away to sea."

The sea-going occurs most often in the twilight hours of evening, but late in the season the last chicks may leave the cliffs at any time of the day. At Cape Hay in 1957, the sea-going was at its peak during the twilight hours of midnight. Salomonsen said that the young leave the Greenland colonies also during the night and Cullen reported a peak of chicks flying during the dusky hours around midnight at Jan Mayen.

There is a great danger to the chicks from predatory gulls during their flight to the sea. Gulls are abundant then, since their own young are on the wing. In addition, migrating hawks and owls are attracted to the colonies at that time. At Akpatok Island in 1954, the number of predators during the sea-going period was nearly double what it had been earlier in the summer. Chicks which go to sea prematurely and would soon perish in any case are preyed upon more frequently than active homoiothermic chicks. Clarke describes such an instance at Spitsbergen: "The looms began to come down from the cliffs at Cape Flora on the 13th of August, and the descent lasted until August 24th. Several old birds came down with one young one; indeed, I have seen as many as five accompany it. It is a bold flight to take, for the cliffs where they are cradled are from 600 to 800 feet above sea-level, and the young birds are not able to sustain their own weight during so long an essay, but gradually come lower and lower until they strike with a heavy thud on the floe or land. Some quickly recover themselves and hurry away as fast as they can to the open water, while others are harried by Burgomasters (*Larus glaucus*); and those that are killed afford food for the bears."

Most murre colonies are so situated that the young can glide directly into the sea. At Akpatok Island, however, between one of the colonies and the sea there was a grassy meadow half a mile in width. Even though the nest ledges were some 500 feet above sea level, very few of the chicks failed to glide directly into the sea.

The habit of going to sea during the twilight hours of evening has definite survival value in that the semi-darkness affords protection from the marauding gulls. Very rarely does a gull attempt to capture a chick surrounded by excited adult murres. There is greater danger to the chick when it is finally led away from the vicinity of the cliffs by the single adult, but as a rule that is done during the darkest part of the night.

FROM *The Murres*

From Another World

LOUIS J. HALLE

It is no use speaking of the great
ocean to the frog in the well.
CHUANG-TZU

A thoughtful naturalist, Louis J. Halle, visits the island of
Mousa, in the Shetlands, with its hidden colony of storm petrels.

ༀ

The birds whose lives are the most remote from human
knowledge are those that spend them far from land in the
wastes of the ocean. Even when they come to land for
breeding, as they must, it may be only at night, and then
only to disappear into underground burrows or fissures of
rock.

Most of us know such birds, if at all, by seeing them from
shipboard. If they are large birds that follow ships, we then
have an opportunity to familiarize ourselves with them in
these limited circumstances. But the birds I am about to

treat of here, although they do follow ships, are the smallest of seabirds. All one sees, ordinarily, is fluttering specks in the trough of the wave.

The order *Procellariiformes* combines an exceptional distinctiveness with a variety exemplified by the fact that it includes both the largest and the smallest of all the seabirds that fly: the Wandering Albatross, with a wingspread of almost twelve feet, and the Storm Petrel, the size of a swallow. In between are a wide assortment of petrels and shearwaters.

On the wing or on the wave the Storm Petrel, only six inches long, appears all black except for a flashing white rump. At sea it dangles its delicate feet to patter over the waves in fluttering flight. When oceanic storms rage for days, with the great combers incessantly crashing along their courses, this little bird somehow survives. Either it must be constantly fluttering in the turbulence without sleep, or it is able to sleep head-under-wing on the tumultuous surface, tossed to the sky, caught in the shattering whitecap, dropped again into the depth of the trough. There is reason to doubt that it makes much distinction between night and day at sea, although it is strictly nocturnal on its breeding grounds.

One of the breeding places is the uninhabited island of Mousa in Shetland. Mousa is less than a mile and a half in its greatest length, hardly more than a thousand yards in its greatest width. A rockbound coast encloses the usual moors of grass, heather, and sphagnum moss, on which sheep and Shetland ponies graze, on which Great Skuas and Arctic Skuas breed; also the usual peat bogs, and a fresh-water loch on which Red-throated Loons raise their young.

This island has, however, a distinction and a fame that have nothing to do with birds. On it is the best preserved of those prehistoric fortresses called "brochs," of which some five hundred are still identifiable in remains scattered over the mainland and the islands of northern Scotland. The birds that are the subject of this chapter, and about which so little can be known, are associated (as we shall see) with the Broch of Mousa, about which virtually nothing is known.

It is a round tower on the coast, forty-three feet high and fifty feet in diameter at its base. It slopes inward in a curve that is convex in its lower half, and slightly concave in its upper, to a summit forty feet in diameter. The construction is of uncut local stones that are, for the most part, naturally flat and no larger than what one could pick up with one hand—a primitive construction lacking cement. Nevertheless, it is tight, its solidity attested by the fact that the broch has endured the high winds of Shetland since the time of Christ. Its wall is some fifteen feet thick at the base, but on the inside it accommodates in its thickness chambers or galleries, as well as a staircase that winds to the summit. (As we shall see, it accommodates more than that in its thickness.) The outside is uniform and unbroken except for one small entrance. Those who took refuge inside could cut themselves off from the world, withstanding its assault.

The Shetlanders incline to believe that the brochs were built by the Picts, but we know virtually nothing about these people whom the Romans encountered over three hundred miles farther south, in Scotland proper, and we have no knowledge that they were ever in these islands.

The same local stones as were used so long ago to build the Broch of Mousa were used in recent times for shoulder-high stone walls in the vicinity of the broch, and for a crofter's house that is falling into ruin now that the island is no longer inhabited. Although these are modern structures, they are of the same construction as the broch.

Visiting the broch in broad daylight one would have no way of knowing that there was life inside the thickness of its wall, or inside the surrounding stone fences. Only by taking the wall apart could one find any evidence of it, but what one then found would be astonishing.

Although Storm Petrels are strictly nocturnal on their nesting grounds, there is no real night in Shetland in July. Instead of darkness there is a dusk that merges into dawn. The sun sets in the northwest about ten o'clock, but the sunset glow remains, moving along the northern horizon until, about four in the morning, now in the northeast, it becomes the sunrise. At the darkest hour, about one, some stars are visible and one can see (as we did on Mousa) a satellite passing north-to-south across the sky. But one could read a book by the light that remains, and the activity of birds is never stilled. All night the gulls and skuas, reduced to silhouettes against the sky, pass overhead crying. All night the Fulmars sweep along the shores or, crossing the island, rise and dip over the contours of its hills.

We had arranged for a boatman to take us to the island at ten in the evening of July 13, 1968, and to come for us again at eight the next morning. The sky was clear of clouds all night and the next day. We walked across the moors from our landing-place, and it was eleven o'clock, with the dusk thickening, when we came to the first of the high stone walls in the vicinity of the broch. Here a low sound pervaded the atmosphere, a continuous and invariable sound that one would say was produced by some small clockwork device with whirring wheels. It was intermediate between the purring of a cat and the softest snoring, all on one pitch but interrupted with perfect regularity, every two or three seconds, by an indescribable single note. One had the impression that it came from a distance until, trying to locate it, one found that, in fact, its source was inside the stone wall only inches away. I could not believe that a bird was inside, producing such a sound. Perhaps an insect, or a small frog.

Mated Storm Petrels relieve each other at the nest every two or, sometimes, three days, the relieved bird spending its leave at sea while the other sits in confinement. We were told that, because they are reluctant to come to land except under cover of true darkness, on cloudless nights at this latitude there are fewer exchanges than usual at the nests. Even well after midnight there was still no sign of such activity. At 12:20, however, standing by a broken-down part of a stone wall from which the buzzing came, we had the impression of a small bird darting into it. A moment later we thought we saw one darting out again (it might have been a Wheatear), and the sound had stopped.

At 12:53, standing by the broch, suddenly we found ourselves surrounded by darting and fluttering shapes. All around the tower, at this darkest hour of the night, was a swarm of what might have been bats—but perfectly silent, with not even a sound from their wings when they almost grazed us. It was hard to make out the features of any individual, since one's eye could hardly follow, in such deep twilight and so near at hand, the swift erratic course of a single bird. They moved for the most part close to the wall, up or down as much as horizontally.

With thousands of undifferentiated chinks between stones, it would be a wonder if any bird could find the one that led to its own nest. Here the utility of the continuous snoring signal became apparent. Some birds seemed to find the right opening at once, whereupon they would quickly squeeze themselves through it, disappearing into the wall. Others were obviously having a hard time. They would flutter vertically up and down the wall, trying to insert themselves into openings that were too small. Sometimes one would, in its flight, swing like a pendulum back and forth along the wall.

One was trying endlessly to find a way into the wall at a place, about three feet above the ground, from which the snoring came. It would cling vertically to the wall with its feet, its wings open and fluttering from moment to moment, its tail spread and the white rump conspicuous, trying to force its head into little openings. One of our party put his hand over it and plucked it from the wall. It was gentle in the hand as we felt the soft depths of its feathered blackness, as we examined the black wires of its feet and the delicately polished black bill—the compound bill, in miniature, of all its order, of the great albatross itself, with an open tube on top. Its jet eye, looking upon us, seemed gentle and indifferent. Released, it darted away, but soon was back, engaged in what seemed a frantic and fruitless search of an area two or three feet square; while, from inside, the mechanical whirring went on without variation. The bird would go away and return to resume the search, which must have continued at least a quarter hour. At last, however, it squeezed itself through an opening and was gone.

Here and there a bird would dart from the wall, always away in a straight line so that there was hardly time to see it. Within minutes of its relief and release it was, one supposes, far out over the open ocean.

The silent swirling of birds all about us continued for over an hour, but now it was getting lighter and the numbers were diminishing. By 2:15 the changing of the guard at the Broch of Mousa was over. Now one would never guess that inside this stone wall was life, that hearts were beating in there. Even the whirring watchworks had stopped.

After we had climbed a hill to see the sunset blossom again, now as sunrise, we returned over the moors to the broch. There it stood in the flooding new light, a monument for tourists, like the Castle of Edinburgh, if it had been accessible to them. One could imagine the official guide, with his patter about the ways of Picts and the features of their architecture, leading his flock through it. The chattering sightseers, and the silent but breathing life hidden in the stone, would still be as far apart as if the former had been in their home towns, the latter skimming the troughs of the mid-Atlantic. Implausible ghosts of reality from an alien world would be listening to tourists, inches away, who could have no inkling of their presence. In the full and disenchanting daylight, however, it was no longer credible that there was a whole strange world of birds inside this dead and silent wall.

Nevertheless, we pursued a certain investigation we had planned. Near the broch, at two separate points where time had crumbled down a stone wall to less than two feet high, we had the previous evening heard the snoring signal. Now, at the first of these points, we lifted off one stone after another until we could see, in a dark recess at ground level, a white egg on a circular bed of grasses. It seemed too large for the egg of so small a bird, and there was no room in the recess, as far as we could see, for a parent bird to be hiding. Touching the egg, however, we found it warm.

Then, while I was setting up tripod and camera for a photographic record, a faint clucking-clicking sound made me turn my eyes to the recess, where a Storm Petrel, a couple of feet from my face, was moving out of nowhere to cover the egg. It settled down and sat watching me.

At the other point along the wall, when the last stone was lifted from over its head, the sitting bird remained on its one large egg, which could be seen under its tail.

After photography we rebuilt the wall over the two sitting birds, each of which remained apparently undisturbed as we posed the stones over it. We belonged to an incomprehensible outer world that they could hardly recognize.

Storm Petrels, by contrast with swallows, know as little of us men as we know of Storm Petrels, by contrast with our knowledge of swallows. I was struck by the fact that they made no move to defend themselves, as other birds do. Even the one we held in our hands did not bite our fingers, and there was no threatening gesture like opening the bill. A larger relative, the Fulmar, which roosts on commanding positions all over Shetland, opens wide its bill to eject a malodorous orange fluid in the direction of any intruder. Storm Petrels, according to the literature, should do likewise, but these did not.

Another observation was of the cleanness of the two nests. We saw little trace of droppings such as one finds in the nests of other species. Since nesting Storm Petrels may go for days without food, even the nestlings, it may be that there is not the same problem of fouling their nests.

The sense of mystery in man is, in the first instance, only an expression of his own ignorance; but secondarily it may be the expression of how great, beyond human comprehension, the world is. Most of us are so preoccupied with our own immediate lives and surroundings that, especially if we live only in cities, we are unaware of all the time and space beyond. There are urgent and wholly absorbing questions of politics, of economic production and trade, of social strife. Philosophers who could well have been born in the cafés of Paris, where they spend their lives, proclaim the doctrine that the world is man's world, that he is the sole creator of any order in it. They can see that this is so by simply looking about them, just as the bee that remains in the hive can, by looking about, see that what it inhabits is a bee-made world.

The Storm Petrel knows our human world only incidentally and along its outermost fringes. In the wide oceans by day and night it sometimes sees a ship passing and follows it, as it would follow a whale, for what it finds in its wake; or it sees an airplane crossing from horizon to horizon; but I would guess that it attaches as little importance to them as the philosopher does to the world outside the city. It knows nothing about man's creation of the world. In its view, the land areas of the earth, on which man works his will, constitute mere rim for the one great ocean that envelops the globe. Even where the birds of Mousa nest, skuas must seem more important than men.

Nevertheless, there is an association, however tenuous. Thousands of years ago, men whom the Parisian philosopher must acknowledge as his forerunners built the abandoned bastion in which these insignificant creatures of the wild continue secretly, year after year, to bring forth their new generations, before they return to the untrodden ocean that, if they were philosophers, they would proclaim as the one and only reality.

FROM *The Storm Petrel and the Owl of Athena*

The Brown Skua

ROBERT CUSHMAN MURPHY

There is hardly a greater contrast between the gentle storm petrel, and the skua, with its hawklike, hooked beak, and piratical behavior. The skuas, of which there are some seven species in two genera, breed in higher latitudes of both the northern and southern hemispheres, having overlapping ranges between them. It may be worth mentioning that the Antarctic skuas undoubtedly reached the South Pole long before human explorers arrived there.

⤙

During the South Georgia Expedition of 1912–1913, I became extremely well acquainted with the Brown Skua, which has left, I believe, a more vivid impression in my memory than any other bird I have met. The skuas look and act like miniature eagles. They fear nothing, never seek to avoid being conspicuous, and, by every token of behavior, they are lords of the far south. In effect, they are gulls which have turned into hawks. Not only are they the enemies of every creature they can master, living almost entirely by ravin and slaughter, but they also have the appearance of a bird of prey in the general color of their plumage, the pointed, erectile hackles on the neck, the hooked bill, and the long, sharp, curved claws, which seem incongruous on webbed feet. They are tremendously strong, heavy, and vital birds which, in the air, look massive rather than speedy. It is therefore somewhat surprising to learn that they can overtake in free flight such swift, long-winged petrels as the Shoemaker (*Procellaria aequinoctialis*). Energy is apparent in every movement of the skua—in its rapacity, in the quantity of food it can ingest within a few moments, and in the volume and continuousness of the screams that issue from its throat. Doubtless, its physiological processes are relatively rapid, even for the group of vertebrates which has the highest metabolic rate. It is therefore not surprising that Valette found the skua's body temperature of 42.3° C. (108.1° F.) to be higher than that of the other warm-blooded animals at the South Orkney Islands.

One usually thinks of the skuas' voice as a scream, because they make their most impressive picture when they stand in angry or defiant attitude, their wings held upright in the posture of those on ancient Norse helmets, and protest with ear-splitting cries. A quieter more conversational note, however, is much like the quacking of a duck and, before I became accustomed to it, I looked for a South Georgian Teal whenever I heard it. I do not remember ever hearing a skua cry out after being wounded by a shot.

The manner in which skuas quickly gather about one of their stoical, injured *confrères,* however, implies neither sympathy nor altruism. It is a good deal of a mystery, in-

deed, as to what sense so quickly leads them to assemble
ominously near a hurt or sickly member of their own tribe,
to follow it about relentlessly if it can still fly, and to stand
by with complete patience until the victim succumbs, or until the moment for the *coup de grace* arrives. Hall states spe-
cifically that skuas have been known to kill and eat their
own wounded mates. I found that they would devour the
flesh of their fellows which I had skinned as avidly as any
other sort of meat. Von den Steinen carried a skua chick to
a distance from its own nest, and when he put it on the
ground it was instantly attacked by all the old birds in the
neighborhood. Brown, Mossman, and Pirie observed a battle almost to the death between two skuas on an ice-floe at
the South Orkneys, while a third bird looked on from an
adjacent hummock. The date was November 9, which suggests that the struggle may possibly have been connected
with courtship. Such contests in nature are rarely fatal, since
supremacy is the only point to be established. In this instance, however, the beaten skua, while too fatigued to defend itself further, was torn to pieces by a Giant Fulmar.

Elsewhere I have spoken of the speed of the skua in
flight, a fact impressed upon me while watching the bulky
birds overhaul and keep pace with Kelp Gulls and various
large petrels, harrying and worrying the victim in an attempt to gain a secondhand dinner. They are always ready
to make themselves annoying and impudent toward any
species, however large. Hall states that even the Black-
browed Albatross will settle in the ocean in order to escape
the molestations of the skua, and they will steal the eggs not
only of the grounded and therefore helpless penguins, but
even those of Wandering Albatrosses and Giant Fulmars.

The skuas were always at hand when the crew of the brig
'Daisy' slew a sea-elephant. The sailors, of course, credited

them with having a keenly developed sense of smell, a sup-
position favored likewise by many naturalists, including
Gain, who has written an account of the South Polar Skua's
uncanny ability to find its way to a scene of blood-spilling.
During the skinning of seals, skuas will sometimes actually
alight on a warm carcass at which men are at work; even
after being repeatedly driven away, they continue to stand
about in a ring only a few steps in diameter.

When mixed flocks of birds were feeding astern of my
anchored vessel, the superior alertness of the skuas over all
other species would become at once apparent. They always
succeeded in getting the lion's share of food tossed over-
board, and would snatch pieces of seal blubber or entrails
practically out of the bills of mollymauks and Giant Fulmars. If a piece of food was dropped in the air by a skua
or any other bird, it was invariably recovered by a skua before it had struck the water. Once a skua alighted on the
mincing table on the deck of the 'Daisy,' where members
of the crew were engaged in cutting up sea-elephant blubber. The bird fed from the edge of the knife, so to speak,
and allowed itself to be touched.

One day when I had killed several King Penguins and
was preparing to skin out their heavy bodies before carrying
the skins across a wide moraine toward my boat, a score of
skuas gathered about me within a few moments, and
crowded forward for the leavings. Several took bits of flesh
and fat from my hand. Pebbles tossed toward them caused
them merely to watch, without any appreciation of the fact
that my gesture might have been menacing. I discharged a
shotgun, with its muzzle held just over their heads, whereupon several of them merely leaped off the ground, and all
ceased their clucking chatter for a few seconds. On this occasion I learned how useful I could make the skuas in clean-

ing the fat from the inside of penguin skins. When the latter, turned inside out, were placed before them, the skuas would pick off the blubber as cleanly as it could have been done with a scraper, and in much less time. They would snip off small bits with the hooks of their beaks, swallowing one after another about as rapidly as a chicken picks up strewn corn. On one occasion I had 35 skuas ready to work, each attempting to perform on my behalf this fundamental and arduous taxidermic process! My helpers battled unendingly, however, even when there was ample room for all, and one or sometimes two old champions monopolized each penguin skin most of the time, to the detriment of efficiency. In fighting, they raised their white-marked wings, and jumped at each other like game cocks, except that they did not use their claws. They knocked each other down in jolly fashion, and pulled out feathers, the battles being half on the ground and half in air. The victor always raised its wings and screamed before turning again toward the banquet and driving off the birds which had slipped into its place. Sometimes three or four of them would grasp one scrap of meat, and pull until it was torn asunder. They would lean back vigorously during such a tug-of-war, bracing their feet far forward and tilting their tails quite to the ground. If one bird flew away with a billful in order to devour it elsewhere, the others would doubtless suspect that he had a superior morsel, for immediately the whole pack would leave its plenteous repast and follow the fugitive, who was sure to be robbed unless he could gulp down his morsel in the air. Their general principle seemed to be that "the far off hills are greener."

Skuas can swallow enormous chunks of food, their throats bulging out bigger than the head during the process. Several of them at South Georgia took in without difficulty

the eye-balls of King Penguins, spheres having the circum-
ference of a half-dollar. To one skua I offered the egg of a
Shoemaker. It promptly took it from my fingers, and swallowed it, shell and all. The average measurements of a score
of eggs of this petrel exceed 83 × 54 millimeters. Loranchet
reports that he once saw a skua at Kerguelen bolt the head
of a rabbit. This introduced mammal has become a regular
part of their food at that island, and skuas have even been
seen to attempt to filch a rabbit out of a dog's mouth.

I have written enough to show that the skuas are the ber-
serkers among birds. They seem to have a diabolical gift to
be a scourge. One day at South Georgia a group of them
pulled open the knot of a fish-trap I had left on the beach,
and dragged out and scattered the bones of a sea-leopard
which the industrious copepods had been cleaning for the
benefit of science. The incomprehensible part of this annoyance was that the trap lay beside the stripped carcass of
a freshly killed sea-elephant upon which a thousand skuas
might have feasted to repletion. But in spite of their vo-
racity, rapine, and cannibalism, the skuas quickly make
themselves the beneficiaries of a peculiar, sentimental, an-
thropomorphic interest. When they crowd around you, and
look up with bright, fearless, unsuspicious, brown eyes, accept the bounty you offer them, and show no more concern
over the loudest shouts, whistles, or handclaps than if they
were stone-deaf, you succumb to their charm, and subscribe
to the principle that their supremacy of might must be deserved.

FROM *The Oceanic Birds of South America*

Emperor Penguins

EDWARD A. WILSON

Edward A. Wilson, a sensitive artist, zoologist, and doctor, accompanied Scott on his Antarctic expeditions. The following extract from his diary was written during the "discovery expedition" of 1901–1904. He died on the second expedition, the "terra nova," 1910–1913, during the party's return from the South Pole.

⟐

First Cape Crozier Journey, 1903

SUN 13 SEPT: Not a bad day at all, though very cold, ranging from −42°F. to −49°F. Yesterday too was cold, ranging from −35°F. to −48°F. As soon as we had had our breakfast of pemmican hoosh, tea and biscuit, Royds, Cross, and I roped and started off to cross the pressure ridges. The other three men we sent over land to have a look at the now deserted Adélie Penguin rookery, some six miles off, where I

wanted them to pick me up a dead bird or two of the year
before with the white throat.

To take our jaunt first. We all had crampons on, iron fit-
tings with long sharp teeth, on our boots of reindeer fur for
climbing the ice. We had one ice axe, which Royds carried
and Cross had a ski pole. I took nothing, as I knew I should
have a load to bring back, or hoped so. We had about two
hours of climbing, stepcutting, dropping into cracks and
crevasses, and hard work in crossing less than half a mile
of these pressure ridges. And then crossing a snow bridge
or two over the narrow end of yesterday's chasm, we eventually descended an easy drift slope on to the new bay ice,
hemmed in here between the rocky cliffs of Cape Crozier
and the ice face of the Barrier proper. This small bay, no
more than five miles long and three deep, is sufficient to
hold in a certain amount of sea ice during the winter, attached to the crumpled Barrier edges.

Beyond the confines of the bay, to the east, there is no
adhesion between the sea ice of Ross Sea and the Barrier
face. Consequently there is constant a lane of open water
along the face of the Barrier cliff, which varies in breadth
with the force and direction of the wind, sometimes closing
entirely and other times opening many miles wide. As we
dropped down on to the bay ice here, we had Ross Sea right
ahead of us, ice covered as far as we could see through the
frost smoke and thick mist, but thin dark ice and many
leads of open water. We could not see more than a few miles
though. On our left towered Mount Terror, coming down
in bumps and rocky conical hills and slopes, interspersed
with snow slopes, running down to a parasitic cone with a
well marked crater called the "Knoll," and the scree slopes
from this Knoll terminate seawards to the north, as well as
Barrier-wards to the east, and northeast in abrupt and mag-

nificent cliffs of columnar basalt, which drop straight down to the bay ice we are standing on, from a height of some five or six hundred feet.

These cliffs form the confines of the little bay to the west, and the top of the cliffs is rocky debris, bare of snow, where they face the sea. But coming back from this edge towards our camp and towards the pressure ridges, other cliffs appear of a similar kind of rock, and these, far from being bare of snow on the top, are capped by precipitous cliffs of the purest blue glacier ice a hundred feet or more in thickness, banded too in a most puzzling way by strata of dirt and rubble, which have been obviously deposited at different times and different periods of level, some sets of strata being worn away at an angle exactly as in the face of ice cliff round Hut Point, close by our winter quarters. This immense ice cliff is falling piece by piece and its fallen ruins, combined with the crushing past of the Barrier ice at the cliff bases, have demolished the pathway down a snow slope that Royds discovered and used the year before, though the prevalence of strong southerly winds, driving through the defile, has already begun to cover up the wreck and prepare another road down, to be destroyed again I suppose by another fall of blue ice from the top of the cliffs.

One thing is very noticeable that on the surface of this blue glacier ice cliff is a mere nothing of névé, so that the ice must have been formed either at a much higher level or at a very remote period of time, under utterly different and far more severe conditions of snow fall and glaciation. Yet it seems there must be some pressure from above, driving these masses of ice over the brow of the precipitous cliffs. There is, as we stand here now, a mass the size of a big hotel split off as a single sérac, poised over the gully of ice ruin and ready to fall.

But to return to the bay ice on which we are standing. In the first place, it is of this winter's growth, for the ice on which Royds stood last year, on which he left two dead Emperor Penguins and a bunch of frozen chicks, has gone out and is replaced by new. It is streaked and splashed in every direction by the droppings of the birds that breed here. These birds, we soon found, had had a scare. For at the point where we descended on to the bay ice, there had been a fall of a large part of the face of the Barrier ice, on to it, crumpling it up and splitting it in all directions, producing a series of mounds and hummocks and a mass of debris, and evidently an uproar which was sufficient to drive away a large group of birds that were huddled together here brooding on their eggs. For here and there around us were these deserted eggs, lying on the ice, or partly buried in the snow and we picked up no less than 16, about a third of which were perfect and unbroken, though all of course were frozen and two thirds of them had split or burst in the process. We found no old birds dead, though some of course may have been buried in the ice fall. Here and there was an egg broken or crushed, showing that the scare had occurred a very little while before the young were hatched, for all that we got were incubated and some were ready to hatch.

This part of the ice was very naturally deserted, and we had to go round a corner of the Barrier edge a few hundred yards to the main colony, which now sat or rather stood under the ice cliff, and not under the rocky cliffs as they did last year. Here we estimated there were altogether about a thousand birds, all standing quietly in one scattered group along the ice face, though I include in this number a few groups that were to be seen standing some two miles out near the open water leads at sea, and a file or two of birds that were coming slowly in towards the rookery one behind the other full of food and covered with ice crystals.

It was amusing to watch these birds when they came to within a hundred yards of the main body. For there they paused and began to clean themselves up most carefully, ridding themselves of the rime and ice crystals that had formed on their handsome feather coats since they left the water. There seemed to me to be no eager clamouring for food among those that had stayed at home, but our presence was disturbing and would have upset the ordinary routine. One cannot say whether these new comers would feed the adults that were nursing chickens, or would take their turn as nurses and allow the others to go and feed, but I imagine the latter is the general procedure, since both male and female are provided with the bare skin and breeding flap for holding and protecting the chick.

There is certainly a community of chicks, for whenever one hurried an adult and made it drop its chick, there was at once a rush for the deserted little one on the part of two or three of the nearest that were unattached, and the winner tucked this windfall into its lap with the appearance of having got what it had wanted for some time. So I think that probably hunger induces a bird to pass on its chicken to someone else while it goes to feed and on returning is perhaps content to join the ranks of the unoccupied until hunger induces the desertion of another chick.

It was a very great surprise to us to find that all the old ones had hatched their eggs and were already nursing chicks apparently every bit as old as those were that Royds and Skelton brought home the year before, on October the 18th, over five weeks later than we are now. I cannot understand this at all, for though among so many birds it is impossible to be certain that none of them were still incubating eggs, we certainly saw nothing but well grown chicks under all that we examined.

One of the most pathetic sights imaginable was to see the parents carrying dead chicks, so strong a desire had they to brood over something. One would see a bird come slowly up to a dead chick that had been dropped by another and edge up towards it, shoving it with its beak towards the lap made by the bird's feet—a platform resting under a very warm lappet of loose skin and feathers. This is evidently a strong instinct, to brood, and it has resulted in the nursing, not only of these dead chicks, which are thus kept from freezing and decompose, losing their down, but also in the incubation of dead and frozen deserted eggs full of dead putrid stuff. We saw several of the penguins moving off with a dead chick, the head and neck trailing out, and when these were dropped sometimes they were appropriated by another bird. Promiscuity seems to be a marked feature and I think each chick must change hands scores of times.

I submitted myself to much vicious pecking and many slaps from the parents' wings in feeling under them for the chicks to see in what position they were carried, and I found the position a happy go lucky one. For the chick lay in any attitude, even on its side across the parents' feet. As a rule however, the bird was crouching with its head down, much as the old bird will sit sometimes all huddled up. The infant has a beautiful silky white and silver grey coat, but is in shape a pot-bellied little thing, with funny clumsy little bigfeet which look as though made of black india rubber. The eyes have a bluish milky look about them, but the iris is seen to be dark brown when examined closely. The bill in life shows no more colour than in the frozen dead chick. The pale markings are white on a black india rubber colour.

Their cry is very shrill and very constant, being an imitation in shrill treble of the inspiratory chuckle of the adult when his head goes down and comes up with a swing. The chick's movements are precisely the same when this shrill whistling trill is emitted.

As regards the power of movement of these penguins when carrying their young, it is always evident from its leg-tied shuffling gait when a bird is hiding and carrying away a chick. The chick is not visible from before or behind, but the head is often seen poking out at one side from under the flap. The adult keeps its feet close together and balances itself well back on the hocks and tail, forming a platform on which the chick lies. And over this falls a bulky fold of loose skin, very heavily feathered except for a hand-palm's space in the middle, where the chick comes closely in contact with the parent's body. It is easily understood therefore that the bird cannot use its feet with freedom, and hence the shuffling gait when it moves along with its chick, in the upright position. If however one hurries the bird's movements at all, down he goes on his breast, and drawing his feet close in under the belly, he holds the chick there and hardly using his feet at all, shoves himself along with his wings and beak, digging them alternately into the snow. In this position it is not long before the chick slips out behind and is left helplessly whistling for a new nurse, an appeal answered like a shot by two or more of the nearest birds unoccupied, who get close up to the deserted chick and seizing it anyhow in their beaks try to shove it into their laps.

In this manoeuvre the chick must often come off second best, and the fact that some of the dead chicks we found have their abdomens rent open, points I think to this energetic fight for the possession of a chick as another cause of mortality among them. We found in all about 30 young dead chicks. Fifteen of these I brought home, the rest I left in a heap on the bay ice. They were all much the same age and size and I suppose the smallest were only just hatched. Among the old Emperors here was a funny tendency to scramble half way up the steep snow slopes that led from the bay ice up to the top Barrier surface. Their foot marks however never went higher than 6 or 8 feet, though it would not have been difficult for the birds to have reached the top.

As to the number of chicks among the adults of this rookery, I put it down at about a hundred or two among the thousand, but it is pure guesswork. For though nothing would have been easier than to get the whole lot on the run and make them drop their chicks for us to count—nothing was harder than to count the birds that were carrying chicks, so well were they hidden away under the feather lappet and so closely was the mass of birds packed—I wanted at all costs to avoid a scare, which might drive them all away and make my next visit in October a fruitless one.

Having seen what we could in the short time we were there, thinking we had another two hours' climb over the pressure ridges to get back to camp we made haste to start. The light had become about as bad as it could be and mist and fog was thickening. We could see nothing of the risky ice ridges we were crossing, except what was just under foot. Royds led with the ice axe, carrying nothing. I followed with a satchel containing all the unbroken eggs, about eight, each as big as a swan's, and in my blouse I had about 15 frozen Emperor chickens, so that I was fairly cumbersome. Cross came after with a net bag of cracked eggs and chicks and a ski pole. We were exceedingly lucky in hitting on a short cut into a drifted valley, which led us back in less than half the time it had taken us to get there.

It was now looking very nasty, with a strong breeze, very

low temperature and a thick white mist blotting out our landmarks rapidly, but we reached our camp at about 4 p.m., a little annoyed to find that the other three whom we had sent over the rock slopes of Terror to the Adélie Penguin rookery had not yet returned. Leaving Cross at the camp, Royds and I at once started off to look for these three, fearing that they might lose their way and miss the camp in the mist. We had gone about two miles, up to the foot of the Knoll when we met them and we all returned together to cook our supper and turn in. Blissett, the marine, arrived in camp with the whole of one side of his face frozen dead white. They were all very foot sore, having had some 4 miles each way over rough stones. However it had been a very satisfactory day's work. I was glad to have the walk up to the Knoll, though it is a part I shall see a great deal more of, on my second visit in October.

There is a very striking feature on the side of the defile in which we camped, on the lower slopes of Mount Terror, in the shape of a sort of raised beach or morainic line, which points perhaps to a considerably higher level in the Barrier surface in previous days of greater glaciation. There are some most interesting erratic boulders of granite all over Mount Terror too, which want a lot of investigation.

MON 14 SEPT: Blissett's face this morning is a sight for sore eyes. He looks as though his two burly tent mates had been sitting on it and so swollen that he can hardly see out of his eye. The weather was no good for more work here. It was not good enough to leave men in camp, for the temperature ranged between −40°F. and −55°F. There was a lot of mist hanging about too and the view out to sea was again of short range owing to mist and frost smoke off the open leads of water.

So we packed up and started for home, the packing of
the eggs and chicks being a very painful business indeed,
during which I got the ends of all my fingers frozen on both
hands. I had every egg packed in paper in one of our large
empty biscuit boxes lashed to the sledge. It was a valuable
cargo. We had to march all day on foot without ski, as the
wind furrows were high and deep, and one man was kept
constantly at the sledge to prevent a capsize. The whole way
home the sledge only capsized once and no damage came
to anything. The weather continued thick and cold and very
uncomfortable all day—no sun. Everyone has very sore feet.

FROM *Diary of the Discovery Expedition*
to the Antarctic: 1901–1904

To the Man-of-War Bird

WALT WHITMAN

This bird of the southern seas was originally called the man-o'-war by the sailors who associated it with swift vessels at full sail. Its current name is "magnificent frigatebird." It has spectacular powers of flight, having a greater wingspread in proportion to its weight than any other bird.

Thou who hast slept all night upon the storm,
Waking renew'd on thy prodigious pinions,
(Burst the wild storm? above it thou ascended'st,
And rested on the sky, thy slave that cradled thee,)
Now a blue point, far, far in heaven floating,
As to the light emerging here on deck I watch thee,
(Myself a speck, a point on the world's floating vast.)
Far, far at sea,
After the night's fierce drifts have strewn the shore with
　　wrecks,

With re-appearing day as now so happy and serene,
The rosy and elastic dawn, the flashing sun,
The limpid spread of air cerulean,
Thou also re-appearest.

Thou born to match the gale, (thou art all wings,)
To cope with heaven and earth and sea and hurricane,
Thou ship of air that never furl'st thy sails,
Days, even weeks untired and onward, through spaces,
    realms gyrating,
At dusk that look'st on Senegal, at morn America,
That sport'st amid the lightning-flash and thunder-cloud,
In them, in thy experiences, had'st thou my soul,
What joys! what joys were thine!

FROM *Complete Poetry & Selected Prose and Letters*

Part Six

The Migrants

The tracks of birds we find in the sand, before they are covered or erased by wind or tide, belong to identifiable species, but where do they lead to? Tierra del Fuego, perhaps, or the Arctic Circle. Long-distance migration, from birds to sea turtles, has long attracted our attention. Something about it not only compels a human mind looking for solutions but tempts our feelings and imaginations in still-untraveled directions across the reaches of the globe. For reasons of climatic and geographical change, or as a result of seasonal shifts in food resources, migration is a dynamic process. Animals, and for that matter plants, continually respond to the ceaseless motion of the planet. Long-distance migrants may follow the same routes for thousands of years, depending on the earth's consistencies, its persistent, rhythmic behavior. Their time scale surpasses our immediate understanding of it. But to stand still is to know the enduring wind, to follow the light, and to sense the greater rhythms of arrival and departure in ourselves.

Migration

PABLO NERUDA

All day, column after column,
a squadron of feathers,
a fluttering airborne
ship
crossed
the tiny infinity
of the window where I search,
question, work, observe, wait.

The tower of sand
and marine space
join there, comprise
song, movement.

Above, the sky unfolds.

So it was: palpitating,
sharp right angles passed

heading northward, westward,
toward open space,
toward the star,
toward the spire of salt and solitude
where the sea casts its clocks to the winds.

It was an angle of birds
steering for
that latitude of iron and snow,
inexorably advancing along
their rectilinear road:
the skyborne numbers
flew with the hungry rectitude
of a well-aimed arrow, winging
their way to procreate, formed
by urgent love and geometry.

I kept looking as far as
the eye could see and saw
nothing but orderly flight,
the multitude of wings against the wind:
I saw serenity multiplied
in that transparent hemisphere
crossed by the obscure decision
of those birds in the firmament.

I saw only the flyway.

All remained celestial.

But among the throngs of birds
homing for their destination
flock after flock sketched out
triangular

victories
united by the voice of a single flight,
by the unity of fire,
by blood,
by thirst, by hunger,
by the cold,
by the precarious day that wept
before being swallowed by night,
by the erotic urgency of life:
the unity of birds
flew
toward the toothless black coasts,
lifeless pinnacles, yellow isles,
where the sun works overtime
and the plural pavilion of sardines
spreads over the warn sea.

On the stone assaulted
by the birds
the secret was set forth:
stone, moisture, excrement, and solitude
will ferment and beneath the blood-red sun
sandy offspring will be born
and they, too, will one day fly back
to the tempestuous cold light,
to the antarctic feet of Chile.

Now they pass, filling the distance,
a faint flapping of wings against the light,
a throbbing winged unity

that flies without breaking

from the migratory

body

which ashore divides,
disperses.

Above the water, in the sky,
the innumerable bird flies on,
the vessel is one,
the transparent ship
builds unity with so many wings,
with so many eyes opened to the sea,
sails over a singular peacefulness
with the movement of one immense wing.

Seabird, migratory foam,
wing from north and south, wave wing,
cluster deployed by flight,
multiplied hungry heart,
you will arrive, great bird, to strip
from the necklace the fragile eggs to be
hatched by the wind and nourished by the sand
until another flight again
multiplies life, death, growth,
wet cries, hot dung,
being born again, and leaving, far
from the windy waste to another windy waste.

Far
from that silence, flee, polar birds,
to the vast rocky silence
and from the nest to the errant number,
sea arrows, bequeath me
the wet glory of time elapsed,

the renowed permanence of feathers
that are born, that die, endure, and throb,
creating fish by fish their long sword,
cruelty against cruelty, the very light
and against the wind and the sea, life.

FROM *Art of Birds* (Jack Schmitt, tr.)

Early Navigation:
By Stars and Birds

In recent years Rachel Carson has become best known for her book Silent Spring, *a lonely and courageous statement against the use of pesticides. But in her earlier books, notably* The Edge of the Sea *and* The Sea around Us, *she encouraged new generations to explore and respect the great oceanic world at our doorstep.*

꙳

So, little by little, through many voyages undertaken over many centuries, the fog and the frightening obscurity of the unknown were lifted from all the surface of the Sea of Darkness. How did they accomplish it—those first voyagers, who had not even the simplest instruments of navigation, who had never seen a nautical chart, to whom the modern miracles of loran, radar, and sonic sounding would have been fantasies beyond belief? Who was the first man to use a mariner's compass, and what were the embryonic beginnings of the charts and the sailing directions that are taken for granted today? None of these questions can be answered with finality; we know only enough to want to know more.

Of the methods of those secretive master mariners, the Phoenicians, we cannot even guess. We have more basis for conjecture about the Polynesians, for we can study their descendants today, and those whose have done so find hints of the methods that led the ancient colonizers of the Pacific on their course from island to island. Certainly they seem to have followed the stars, which burned brightly in the heavens over those calm Pacific regions, which are so unlike the stormy and fog-bound northern seas. The Polynesians considered the stars as moving bands of light that passed across the inverted pit of the sky, and they sailed toward the stars which they knew passed over the islands of their destination. All the language of the sea was understood by them: the varying color of the water, the haze of surf breaking on rocks yet below the horizon, and the cloud patches that hang over every islet of the tropic seas and sometimes seem even to reflect the color of a lagoon within a coral atoll.

Students of primitive navigation believe that the migrations of birds had meaning for the Polynesians, and that they learned much from watching the flocks that gathered each year in the spring and fall, launched out over the ocean, and returned later out of the emptiness into which they had vanished. Harold Gatty believes the Hawaiians may have found their islands by following the spring migration of the golden plover from Tahiti to the Hawaiian chain, as the birds returned to the North American mainland. He has also suggested that the migratory path of the shining cuckoo may have guided other colonists from the Solomons to New Zealand.

Tradition and written records tell us that primitive navigators often carried with them birds which they would release and follow to land. The frigate bird or man-of-war bird was the shore-sighting bird of the Polynesians (even in recent times it has been used to carry messages between islands), and in the Norse Sagas we have an account of the use of 'ravens' by Floki Vilgerdarson to show him the way to Iceland, 'since seafaring men had no loadstone at that time in the north . . . Thence he sailed out to sea with the three ravens . . . And when he let loose the first it flew back astern. The second flew up into the air and back to the ship. The third flew forward over the prow, where they found land.'

In thick and foggy weather, according to repeated statements in the Sagas, the Norsemen drifted for days without knowing where they were. Then they often had to rely on observing the flight of birds to judge the direction of land. The *Landnamabok* says that on the course from Norway to Greenland the voyager should keep far enough to the south of Iceland to have birds and whales from there. In shallow waters it appears that the Norsemen took some sort of soundings, for the *Historia Norwegiae* records that Ingolf and Hjorleif found Iceland 'by probing the waves with the lead.'

FROM *The Sea around Us*

How Birds Migrate

ROGER J. PASQUIER

This clearly written summary of the phenomenon of bird migration details some of the efforts made to solve its mysteries.

Recently, scientific evidence has suggested that birds are impelled to leave their wintering grounds, regardless of the equal length of day and night. The internal timing needed to start a bird on its migration seems to be based on an internal, so-called endogenous rhythm, which acts like a biological clock, similar to that which has been found in many other animals. Annual rhythms in the birds correspond to the seasons and the solar year. Thus their internal state tells them which direction to follow and how far, although they are able to adjust to changing conditions along the way. The wheeling of the earth under the sun is part of their innate experience.

The manner in which each species migrates reflects its needs and capabilities as closely as does its route and destination. The vast majority of birds fly, of course, but other species will swim or walk to their destination: several species of penguin swim north every year after breeding on Antarctic or sub-Antarctic islands, and even some strong fliers such as grebes, brant geese, eider ducks, and murres swim considerable distances. In North America the Common Turkey used to migrate great distances on foot as well as by flight; with the clearing of the eastern forests this is no longer possible.

The mystery of migration has always been heightened by the fact that many birds are never seen actually migrating. Birds that migrate at night baffled earlier observers, who could not account for their sudden appearances or disappearances, and today, with sophisticated scientific equipment, night migrants are still very difficult to study. Long flights pose hazards at any time, but for some species certain hours offer advantages which outweigh the dangers involved; others migrate during both light and dark hours, and many of the birds that usually fly during one period occasionally make such long flights that light or darkness overtakes them where they cannot stop, such as over the Gulf of Mexico.

What are some of the advantages of day and night travel, and to which birds might it make no difference? The majority of night migrants are the small land birds that travel great distances to the tropics and are ordinarily considered weak fliers; by flying at night they avoid being visible to hawks, gulls, and other birds that could easily catch them. Another advantage of night flight is that it allows all the daylight hours for feeding and rest; small birds burn up energy so quickly that after a night spent flying they must feed again, even before resting. Since these birds cannot fly as fast as some day migrants, but often have farther to travel,

if they flew only in daylight in addition to feeding and resting, their migrations would take much longer, perhaps
more time than the seasons allow, so for them flying at night
is a much more efficient system.

Night migrants cannot usually be seen, but they can
often be heard: many of the small birds periodically chirp;
on a quiet night in April or May, or late August, September,
or October, the sky may be filled with call notes that can be
identified as to family, if not to species. The calls must help
birds avoid collisions and indicate the number of birds
nearby, although they cannot communicate any navigational information. On nights when the moon is full, birds
can sometimes be seen traveling across it—try focusing on
the moon with binoculars or a telescope; some larger species, like geese, can be identified by their profile.

Daytime migrants include the small birds that can feed
as they fly, such as swifts and swallows, which catch aerial
insects while traveling, combining two activities that are
separate for most birds; moreover, they are fast enough fliers
that they needn't make special efforts to avoid predators, as
some small birds must. Other small daytime migrants include various finches and blackbirds, somewhat protected
by flying in flocks and not forced to budget their time as
tightly as the night migrants, since they are not traveling so
far.

Many of the larger birds, such as hawks and herons,
which often utilize thermals to keep them aloft with little
or no expenditure of their own energy, must migrate during
the day, because thermals exist only in the daytime and over
land. To utilize these, some birds must increase their travel
distance: the White Stork of Europe, for example, has a
gliding flight that takes advantage of rising and falling air
currents; it avoids flying over bodies of water like the Med-

iterranean, making long detours west to Spain to cross the Mediterranean at Gibraltar, or east to Turkey and Israel to avoid it entirely, before going south into Africa, while the European Crane, a bird of approximately the same size, flaps rather than glides, and is independent of air currents, taking a much shorter route across the Mediterranean at its widest point.

Still other birds, including ducks, geese, shorebirds, terns, and seabirds, travel both in the day and at night. They are strong fliers; some, like the American Golden Plover, have routes that require continuous travel over periods longer than those of light or darkness, and others, like the petrels and shearwaters that travel across the oceans, live in environments with hazards and benefits equal during day and night.

Weather conditions play a role in a bird's decision to migrate on any particular day or night. The weather factors influencing this decision are complicated, but obviously it is harder for a bird to travel in a violent rainstorm, in dense fog obscuring landmarks and hazards, or when strong winds might blow it off course; birds are found migrating in all these conditions, especially when they develop after the bird has begun flying, but birds usually try to take advantage of weather conditions that make flight easier. Most spring migrants move north with a warm front and seem to prefer a slight tail wind; fall migrants move south with a cold front and a north or northwest wind. Some larger birds fly most easily with a head wind, gaining support as a kite does—at Hawk Mountain Sanctuary in Pennsylvania, where large numbers of hawks pass every fall, taking advantage of the thermals created by the long series of mountain slopes, the greatest flights are seen when sunny local conditions combine with northeast or northwest winds and a depression moving east from the Great Lakes.

Birds travel at the heights and speeds that suit their requirements. Studies with radio transmitters attached to birds, with radar, and from airplanes indicate that most of the small night migrants fly below 5000 feet, and the majority between 2000 and 3000, but flocks of shorebirds are regularly detected by radar at 20,000 feet. The shorebirds are traveling great distances without stopping and may find favorable winds at that altitude. Sea ducks such as eiders and scoters fly just over the surface of the water, but rise higher over land, while land birds often fly higher over the sea. Flocks of blackbirds, jays, and finches sometimes fly just over the trees, while hawks riding thermals rise several thousand feet, beyond human vision. The highest altitude record is probably held by the Bar-headed Goose, which regularly flies at 30,000 feet to pass over the highest Himalayan peaks.

The rates at which birds travel is highly variable: some travel faster or longer during certain stages of migration, while many night migrants do not travel the entire night, and most spend a few days feeding and resting between flights. The migration of most small birds between the tropics and North America takes several weeks or months, but an altitudinal migration may be accomplished in a day. The Blackpoll Warbler, which flies from South America over the Caribbean to Cuba and Florida before spreading over North America, averages about 30 miles per day (but more per flight, since it does not fly every night) over the United States, but accelerates to 200 miles per day as it approaches its sub-Arctic breeding grounds; perhaps if its average speed were faster it would arrive north too early. In spring, many birds have to travel at a pace that is not faster than the northward progress of spring itself; sometimes insectivorous birds traveling north encounter a late cold snap, and may perish by the thousands if the weather kills their insect prey or delays its hatching.

Birds making long flights usually move at greater speeds: American Golden Plovers flying from Nova Scotia to northern South America, for example, usually make the 2400-mile trip in 48 hours, for an average speed of 50 miles per hour, and a marked Peregrine Falcon that escaped near Paris was recovered 24 hours later at Malta, 1350 miles away. Snow Geese make long nonstop flights between their Arctic breeding grounds and wintering areas on the Gulf coast; some flights are more than 2000 miles, but the actual speeds are unknown.

Data from banding stations have been extremely valuable in plotting the speeds and courses of individual birds and have also revealed migration patterns that could not be discovered except by examining large numbers of birds in the hand. It is now well known that different populations of some species winter in different areas; female and immature Dark-eyed Juncos, for example, travel farther south than adult males, and immature Herring Gulls move less far south each year as they approach maturity. Banding data have also shown that different parts of the population may use different routes or schedules to reach the same destination. One such example of differential migration comes from a comparison of captures at coastal and inland banding stations: at stations on the Atlantic coastline and offshore islands, a very high percentage of fall passerine migrants are immature birds, while at inland stations the number of adult migrants may approach 50 percent, a more accurate part of the total population. It has been suggested that the more experienced adult birds take a slightly inland route, to avoid the dangers of being blown out to sea, while the immature birds, making the trip for the first time, fail to compensate for winds that drive them seaward.

Another aspect of differential migration involves adults and immatures migrating at different times in fall: at the Carnegie Museum's banding station east of Pittsburgh, it was found that the peak of adult movement for Red-eyed Vireos and White-throated Sparrows preceded that of immatures by ten days, and adult Dark-eyed Juncos preceded immatures by two weeks, but for Nashville and Magnolia Warblers, the bulk of immatures preceded adults by ten days; no explanation for this has yet been found.

The most amazing and mysterious aspect of bird migration is navigation. How can birds traveling long distances, often in the dark, keep on a regular course and, in some cases, find their way back to exactly the same breeding or wintering spot used in previous years? What about the immature birds, often traveling alone, on their first trips? As we have seen, in some species the inexperienced birds fail to avoid the riskier route along the coast, and most of the out-of-place vagrants found in fall throughout the country, but particularly on the coasts, are immatures—disoriented western birds that have wandered to the Atlantic and Gulf coasts and eastern birds on the Pacific coast—but obviously the bulk of the first-time migrants must reach their proper destinations, or the species wouldn't survive.

Our appreciation of the navigational ability of birds has been considerably increased by experiments that have taken birds away from areas they normally traverse on migration, in which they could be expected to orient successfully. The most famous of these experiments were performed by Lockley on Manx Shearwaters nesting on the island of

Skokholm off Wales. Shearwaters released in Venice and Switzerland were back in their nest burrows in fourteen days; whether the shearwaters took the most direct route, by flying overland (something shearwaters never ordinarily do) or returned through the Mediterranean, the trips were over areas previously untraveled by Manx Shearwaters. In another experiment, a Manx Shearwater was released at Boston, 3050 miles from home, in another area unknown to the species; this bird was back in twelve and a half days. Similar experiments have demonstrated that several other seabirds, which normally travel far over the seas, have excellent navigational abilities, but many small land birds do as well—wintering White-crowned and Golden-crowned Sparrows returned to California from release points in Louisiana and Maryland.

Birds use several things to guide them, and most birds are capable of using more than one navigational system. The most obvious are geographical landmarks. Most birds that migrate at all move about to a certain extent within their breeding area and could recognize it from this experience when they returned the following year. Leaving the breeding area, day-flying birds could continue to follow geographical features such as river valleys, mountain ranges, coastlines, etc., most of which run, in North America, in the same directions that most migrants travel. Night migrants are of course active during the day, and may recognize landmarks as they near their destination.

By a series of experiments with Starlings in the 1940s and 1950s, the German ornithologist Gustav Kramer demonstrated that birds use the sun for navigation. Kramer observed first the behavior of Starlings kept in cages where they could see only the sun; in autumn the birds displayed "migratory restlessness," hopping and beating against the side of the cage, with most of the movement in the southwest side of the cage, the direction in which the Starlings would be migrating. In spring, the Starlings' restlessness was directed at the northeast side of the cage. By using mirrors, Kramer showed that the Starlings needed only to see the light, not the sun itself, to orient correctly—this is an important ability for birds, since the sun is often obscured by clouds. In experiments with artificial cloud effects, the birds became confused, but were able to reorient instantly whenever a short flash of light came through. When Kramer used mirrors to deflect the sunlight 90 degrees, the Starlings reoriented in terms of the light's new, unnatural direction, but other experiments showed they had an internal clock that compensated for the sun's normal movement through the sky.

Night migrants can use the position of the sun at dusk to get an initial direction, but they must use other means to maintain a steady course. Experiments by Stephen Emlen of Cornell University have shown how Indigo Buntings, and possibly other birds, use the stars. Emlen placed the buntings in individual cages made of a white blotting paper funnel mounted over an ink pad, so that every time the birds hopped on the blotting paper their feet left a mark; by counting the number of footprints in each part of the paper, he could determine the direction in which most movement took place. In the first experiments, out of doors, Emlen found that in autumn Indigo Buntings exhibiting migratory restlessness hopped mainly in the south part of their cages; under partially overcast conditions most continued to orient correctly. Brought into a planetarium where they were shown simulated fall skies, the buntings oriented correctly, but when the skies were reversed 180 degrees, the buntings similarly reversed their direction, remaining consistent with the stars.

By reducing the number of stars shown in the planetarium, Emlen learned which are important for navigation: he found that in both spring and fall the entire southern half of the sky could be eliminated without affecting the buntings' navigational abilities; removal of the Milky Way, Big Dipper, and North Star had little effect, but when all the northern stars were eliminated, even with the southern stars visible, orientation became random. If all the stars were eliminated, replaced by a diffuse light, orientation further deteriorated, and most birds ceased activity, which suggests that sight of the stars may, in the proper season, itself stimulate migration.

Ability to use the stars for navigation apparently varies among individual birds and between species and families, since among Emlen's buntings, different birds seemed to orient more accurately when shown different sets of stars, although they always oriented according to the actual season whether they were shown a spring or fall sky. In similar experiments, Old World warblers oriented according to the season of the sky they were shown; because migration has developed independently in different groups of birds, we might expect different uses or interpretations of the stars and other environmental stimuli.

Since birds sometimes migrate when weather conditions prevent them from receiving clues from either the sun or the stars, they must have other indicators also. In these cases wind direction may be an aid, especially at times when clouds obscure celestial features that were visible when the birds took off, but the wind continues from the same direction. The sounds of waves on shores, streams, wind through the trees, or animal life on the ground may be used by birds—the writings of early balloonists, who heard such sounds while traveling quietly at great altitudes, have been used to show that these sounds could also be heard by birds; sounds could certainly tell them the habitat over which they are flying, and the sounds of waves breaking on a beach would be a valuable indicator to birds approaching land or trying not to leave it.

In addition to knowing how to reach their destination, birds must also know when to travel. A too-early spring departure may make birds arrive on their breeding grounds before enough food is available, and starting too late may mean missing the best season for beginning the nesting cycle. Similarly a too-early departure in fall may bring birds to their wintering areas at an inappropriate time, and by waiting too long they may be overtaken by the effects of cold weather.

Since so many birds arrive in and depart from their nesting areas at the same time every year, irrespective of day-to-day weather conditions, the sense of time seems to be independent of changeable environmental circumstances. For many birds, the initial migratory stimulus may be changes in day length; laboratory experiments have shown that some birds exposed to artificial changes in day length will assume the physiological state appropriate to the season the lights reproduce: thus, birds given increased amounts of light will develop the glandular characteristics of a bird ready to breed, and, if a nocturnal migrant, will hop and beat mainly against the northern wall of its cage in a state of migratory restlessness after dark, whether it is actually spring or not. However, it is not known whether the glands that have been stimulated by increased day length, in experiments or real situations, actually stimulate migratory urges or simply occur at the same time. If changes in day length indeed stimulate migrants, for those Northern Hemisphere birds wintering south of the Equator the stimulus must be decreasing day length in both spring and fall. Of course, this theory does not account for the development of migratory urges in the birds that winter in the equatorial zone of fairly constant day length; this is a subject on which much work remains to be done.

FROM *Watching Birds*

The Rainbow Birds
of Spring

EDWIN WAY TEALE

A dedicated naturalist follows the wave of warblers, "warblers beyond counting," as they fly north and overland from Central and South America during the peak of their spring migration. They add their bright colors to the fresh green leaves starting to cover the land.

☙

During the night a great warbler wave had poured over the Appalachians, spilling its gay, colorful migrants down the ridges that, in gigantic waves of granite, descended toward the east. The fluttering wings that had carried them from islands of the Caribbean, from Central or South America, from Mexico, had lifted them over the barrier of this ancient range. Before we had started our trip, Ludlow Griscom, Harvard's famed field ornithologist, had told us:

"Be near Asheville, North Carolina, the third week in April and you will see the warblers pour across the mountains."

This was the third week in April. And these were the warblers he had promised. Nearly one-third of all the species of warblers found east of the Rockies were about us that day.

We never knew whether we were in the beginning, the middle, or the end of the wave. We drove for more than a hundred miles, from east of Asheville south to Hendersonville and west to Highlands, and there were warblers, pockets of warblers, trees swarming with warblers, warblers beyond count, along the way. These rainbow birds of spring, like other manifestations of spring, increased and decreased as our road tobogganed or climbed. They were most numerous in the valleys; absent almost entirely on the higher summits. Wood warblers come north as the leaves unfold. They feed on the forest caterpillars that feed on the new green leaves. Their northward flight keeps pace with unfolding bud and expanding leaf. The sequences of nature, the timing of the tides of migration, are exact. Buds burst, new leaves unfurl, larvae hatch, and warblers appear.

South of Asheville the road descended a long decline with climax forest on either side. For an hour we swept the hardwoods with our glasses, watching the warbler show.

No other family of North American birds travels more in mixed companies than do the wood warblers. Redstarts darted among the branches, fanning their brilliant tails. Ovenbirds called from the woodland floor. Prairie warblers endlessly went up the scale in the thin "zee-zee-zee-zee-zee-

zee" of their song and chestnut-sided warblers ended on a whiplash "switch you!" As they appeared and disappeared among branches and bushes, we saw the rich lemon of yellow warblers, the black raccoon masks across the faces of Maryland yellowthroats, the flash of yellow rump patches as myrtle warblers swooped and rose. We watched hooded warblers opening and closing their tails—birds that to Frank M. Chapman seemed to say: "You must come to the woods, or you won't see me!" The final notes are almost as explosive as those of the chestnut-sided. High in the oaks and maples the parula, smallest of all North American warblers, hung from twig tips like a chickadee or flashed among the new leaves the brilliance of its yellow throat and breast, its white wing bars, and the old-gold shield on its bluish back. And every bird was in perfect plumage. This was the season of the new and unmarred leaf, the time of the bird at its best. This was the unblemished world of the spring.

A little later we pulled up near a huge tulip tree. Its billowing cloud of pale-green new leaves was a world of succulent plenty for larva and warbler alike. Magnolia warblers and black-throated blues and parulas and redstarts and myrtles swarmed through this arboreal land of plenty. Nothing in the world is more alive than a warbler in the spring. Surely it must have been a warbler that James Stephens described in *The Crock of Gold* as being "so full of all-of-a-sudden." All of a sudden a warbler starts and stops. All of a sudden it flashes from branch to branch, peers under leaves, snaps up small caterpillars, darts on again.

One black-and-white warbler, a little striped mouse of a bird, left its caterpillar hunting to hawk after a pale-brown moth gyrating beyond a lower branch. It fluttered, hovered, spurted ahead, missed the moth in its erratic course time after time. In the end it became discouraged and suddenly zoomed upward, back to the trunk among the gray-green leaves of the tulip tree. By the time we drove on, our necks ached from looking up at the strenuous little treetop birds.

In the White House, in Washington, D.C., on May 4, 1906, Theodore Roosevelt wrote to John Burroughs, at Slabsides, that he had just come in from walking around the White House grounds and had wished heartily that Burroughs had been there to tell him what the various warblers were. Most of the birds had been in the tops of the trees and he could not get good glimpses of them. But there was one with chestnut cheeks, with bright yellow behind the cheeks and a yellow breast thickly streaked with black, which had puzzled him.

This same warbler that perplexed the twenty-sixth President of the United States at the White House danced among the upper branches of a maple near the cemetery at Fletcher, North Carolina, where Bill Nye, the humorist, is buried. It was a Cape May warbler, the only one with chestnut cheeks. This warbler, incidentally, has little to do with Cape May, New Jersey. It does not breed there. I have never seen one there. Its name resulted from the fact that, during migration in 1809, the individual from which it was described happened to be shot on Cape May. Breeding almost as far north as the Great Slave Lake of northern Canada, these warblers concentrate in winter in the West Indies, especially on the island of Haiti. The path of their migration is wide at the top and funnels down to form, roughly, an inverted pyramid.

In contrast, the redstart—the "firetail," the warbler the Cubans call the "little torch"—has a particularly broad front throughout both its southward and its northward movement. As these warblers near their southern wintering grounds, their flyway still has a width of more than two thousand miles, extending all the way from Mexico on the west to the Bahamas on the east.

Near Druid Hills, North Carolina, we pulled up beside an apple orchard in bloom. The trees descended a long slope to tumbling clouds of white. Bees hummed. The air was fragrant with the perfume of the apple blossoms. Sunshine filtered among the branches, where a myriad white petals glowed, luminous in the backlighting. And here warblers—myrtles, magnolias, Maryland yellowthroats, prairies, and black-and-whites—darted amid blossom-laden boughs or flicked, in flashes of living color, from tree to tree.

There were other moments of especial beauty that day. Where a mountain road turned sharply on the way to Highlands, a black-and-white warbler flitted past us over a shining, glittering waterfall of mica that streamed down an embankment from decomposing rock. Then there was the hooded warbler we saw, singing with face lifted to the sunny sky, beside an upland pasture blue with bird's-foot violets. Once we came upon a prairie warbler, its yellow breast edged with streakings of black and its tail bobbing about, balancing itself on the fiddlehead of a cinnamon fern. Another time a long finger of sunshine descending through a treetop spotlighted a Maryland yellowthroat, brilliant in contrasting yellow and black, swinging on a low cluster of red maple keys.

John Burroughs thought the yellowthroat's song said: "Which way, sir? Which way, sir? Which way, sir?" In a less genteel modern day it is usually set down as: "Wichity,

wichity, wichity, witch." And so it sounds in the North. But here some of the birds seemed substituting an "s" sound; seemed to be singing: "Seizery, seizery, seizery." We wondered if this was a warbler dialect, a local accent given by birds that originated in the same area. Several times on our trip we encountered regional variations in song.

FROM *North with the Spring*

Migration of the Shorebirds

PETER MATTHIESSEN

Did you ever chance to hear the midnight flight of
birds passing through the air and darkness overhead,
in countless armies, changing their early or late summer
habitat? It is something not to be forgotten. . . . You
could hear . . . "the rush of mighty wings," but oftener
a velvety rustle, long drawn out . . . occasionally from
high in the air came the notes of the plover.

WALT WHITMAN, *Specimen Days*

*The author of this selection describes in clear detail the migra-
tion of restless shorebirds, which often fly astounding distances
to reach their nesting grounds. Fitting great distances and a
short season together in their minds, these fast flyers seem to reflect the spinning of the earth itself.*

———

The wind birds are strong, marvelous fliers, averaging greater distances in their migrations than any other bird family on earth. Of the several hundred migratory birds of North America, only thirty-five winter as far south as central Chile, and in this group the barn swallow, blackpoll warbler, and Swainson's thrush, the osprey, broad-winged hawk, and peregrine, with a few gulls, fly that far only irregularly. All the rest of the thirty-five are shorebirds, several of which go all the way to land's end, near Cape Horn. The white-rumped sandpiper, which flies nine thousand miles twice every year in pursuit of summer, is only exceeded in the distance of its north-south migration by the Arctic tern, and the golden plover far exceeds the tern in the distances covered in a single flight; it is thought to travel well over two thousand miles nonstop on both its Atlantic and Pacific migrations. The bristle-thighed curlew, which flies from Alaska to Polynesia and New Zealand, is another distance flier of renown; and so are the ruddy turnstone, wandering tattler, and sanderling, which may be found on the most far-flung strands and atolls throughout their enormous range.

Because of the great distances they must travel, the migrants make preparations to depart again within a few months of their arrival from the north; the flocking and reflocking that is evident on the summer coasts and pampas of the Southern Hemisphere is a symptom of premigratory restlessness. This restlessness is not entirely attributable to activity of the glands, for castrated birds will migrate, borne along, perhaps, by the northward tide of movement. Migration is part of an annual cycle which also includes breeding and molt; what is not yet fully known is the exact pattern of stimuli, physiological and/or external, that puts this cycle into motion.

Temperature, which was long assumed to be the controlling factor, is now thought to have no effect at all, but it is generally agreed that the onset of warm weather, with an increased food supply and a lessened heat loss, gives the bird the excess energy which is expressed in migration and reproduction. Food supply, light intensity, seasonal rains, and many other forces, including internal rhythms of the glands, may help incite the reproductive dance, but the strongest goad of all appears to be reaction to a change in light as the season turns; this reaction, in both plants and animals, is called photoperiodism. The intensity of illumination, however, is probably less important than the longer day in which to remain active. "Daylight probably stimulates gonads not because it is beneficial to general well-being, but because a physiological timing mechanism has been evolved between gonad development and an external factor associated with spring." Thus, birds which winter in the West Indies or the southern states are thought to be stirred in early spring by the lengthening of the days.

But the spotted sandpiper may fly to the region of the equator, where day length is constant throughout the year; and where the white-rumped sandpiper winters in the uttermost part of the earth, the summer days of February, far from lengthening, grow shorter with the advent of the Capricornian autumn. Unless they possess some internal chronometer quite independent of external stimuli, the equatorial migrants must be awakened from the sameness of their days by some such phenomenon as a change in the rains or the northerly drift of the sun, while the species wintering in austral latitudes may be stirred by the *shortening* of days toward such activities as song, mock fighting, and formation of pairs which are the external symptoms of pituitary change.

By February, in Tierra del Fuego, male white-rumped sandpipers are already engaged in mock battles with other males of their own kind. The birds circle like midget roosters, leaping up and down with sexual rage, but never touching. Their mock flights are a sign not of distaste for their own kind but of an impulse to perpetuate it; the time of premigration courtship has begun. On the northern continent, a few woodcock have already begun to nest; the snipe and killdeer, in late February, would be winging northward, crowding the retreat of frozen earth.

The gland quickening and fat accumulation which encourage the white-rump's hypertonic belligerence also produce a symptom known as *Zugunruhe,* or migration restlessness, which is confined to migratory birds; many shorebirds travel through the night, and a wild bird held captive in its time of passage will sleep for a short time after sunset, then become more and more fretful until nearly midnight, when the fever of flight begins to taper off. *Zugunruhe,* which is inhibited in spring by a turn of cold weather and in autumn by a spell of warmth, is ordinarily accompanied by compass orientation: if placed outdoors where it can see the stars, the captive will face north in spring and southward in the fall.

The urge to migrate is strongest in birds of the cold climes of the northern continent, where seasonal changes in climate are most pronounced; a few austral species migrate *south* to breed, returning northward to escape Antarctic winter (the lesser seed snipe nests in Tierra del Fuego and winters in central Argentina, while the Magellanic snipe winters north to Uruguay), but the migrations are much shorter, for the range in temperature is less.

Migration routes apply more rigidly to species than to the individual shorebird, which may adjust its heading and even its route and destination from year to year, depending on whim and circumstance. But the piping plover, ruddy turnstone, and sanderling have been known to return to the same nesting ground, in what is known as *Ortstreue* or "place faithfulness," and spotted sandpipers—presumably the same pair—have occupied the identical nest site in consecutive years. A stilt sandpiper banded at Hudson's Bay also returned the next year to the same scrape, and possibly *Ortstreue* occurs in shorebirds generally.

As the time to migrate nears, the shorebirds rise and form huge flocks and veer apart in small ones, accumulating in the air again like bits of mercury, alighting for a quick moment before breaking away anew. They are frantic to be off, yet the last impulse has not come that will whirl them from the shore and send them spinning to the altitudes, perhaps three miles in the air, that are best suited to the spanning of the earth.

A meteorological signal may release them. Electricity in the air affects the migration behavior of curlews, oystercatchers, and others, though these effects are not well understood. And unlike birds of fixed migration dates, such as certain swifts and swallows, shorebirds may be delayed a month or more by high-pressure areas to the north. This indicates that the migration impulse, however strong, is not likely to run away with the bird in the face of adverse conditions.

On the other hand, bad weather encourages the flock instinct in birds by inhibiting spring sexuality and belligerence: "the factors which are associated with increased flocking are those that may be considered unfavorable." Cold or famine or the dangers of migration tend to draw the birds together: as social creatures, they need one another, and in hard times the need triumphs over the seasonal intolerance brought on by awakening hormones. Therefore, the wind birds are flocked and ready to be off when the first pale band of light breaks the horizon.

Most birds of open spaces are gregarious by nature, as if otherwise, in the vastness of a world where all horizons are so distant, they would be little more than wind-blown scraps. The flock, with its cumulative sense of direction, serves as protection for individuals against straying off into infinities; a tired bird can benefit by the experience of the leaders. It is also a defense against the predators; hawks seem daunted by the unity or just plain bulk of a close flock. (This phenomenon has been well described in regard to schools of fish—the "mystical sort of protective anonymity, thought to confound a predator unable to concentrate its hunger on any one of such a host.") Most shorebirds, like ducks and other birds, cluster together in time of peril, and white-rumped sandpipers may rush at a predator in a body and scatter in its face in a "confusion" attack which usually turns it aside.

The ruddy turnstone, though it migrates in small groups, "is not particularly sociable. . . . I have occasionally observed a marked hierarchy in a party of only two birds, the inferior individual avoiding the superior one." And the Wilson's plover, in company with the snipe and woodcock, the spotted sandpiper, and most of the tattlers (the lesser yellowlegs is an exception), is a casual flocker at best. The solitary sandpiper, even if apprehended in a group, will scatter when it takes flight—entirely unlike the great majority of sandpipers, whose habit of snapping together in the air like magnets was of no small convenience to the gunner in the days when they were shot. Some nonflockers have either a short migration span or inland habitats where flocking would be a nuisance, but the greater yellowlegs may keep its own company all the way from Tierra del Fuego to Alaska.

Then the flocks are gone. On tide flats which at twilight of the evening past had swarmed with shorebirds, dirtied feathers drift across white-spotted mud, and hard shreds of dried algae, and brown spindrift, and the husks of dead crustaceans. The solitary birds that pass look forlorn and indecisive, and in the emptiness their calls receive no answer. These are the sick, weak, injured, and immature, whose impulses were not strong enough to hurl them upward at the northern stars; now they must wait out the southern winter. Greater and lesser yellowlegs are common birds in the Argentine throughout the year, and the Hudsonian godwit was once so widespread on the pampas from April to September that naturalists of eighty years ago called them a population of "Antarctic" breeders.

Left behind on ocean coasts from Panama to California and New England are those individuals whose energies got them underway but did not drive them to complete their journey. These birds—the ones seen in the northern states on the beaches of late June—may have set out with their fellows out of pure sociability, for birds, like dogs and men, are drawn to movement. On June 26, 1964, there was a flock of thirty-odd black-bellied plover on the ocean beach a few miles from Sagaponack; despite the surprising number, one must assume that all these were nonbreeders, for this plover nests within the Arctic Circle.

Because of the pressures of the breeding cycle, spring migration is performed much more rapidly than migration in the fall. Northbound dunlin, passing a light plane, have been timed at 110 miles per hour, or nearly twice the usual recorded flight speeds of other shorebirds. Birds, when pressed, are capable of a sharp increase in velocity, and in the thin air of high altitudes, migrants probably travel at a rate rarely attained nearer the ground. The bristle-thighed curlew flies the six thousand miles or more from New Zealand to its nesting grounds in western Alaska in about six weeks, while the southward journey may take twice as long. Birds winging northward from the Argentine move with corresponding haste. There appear to be few feeding grounds on the muddy coasts of northern South America and in the almost tideless Caribbean, and the golden plover may sometimes fly from the beaches of Peru all the way to the Gulf Coast without alighting. (The bladder snail *Physa* has been found in both crop and plumage of certain migrant plover, encouraging the startling idea that these birds might deliberately place snails in their plumage before starting on a long voyage in order to provide themselves with at least one meal during the trip.)

By late March and early April, when the wind birds appear in the big skies of the Gulf of Mexico, the killdeer, snipe, and woodcock that wintered on the Gulf Coast may already have flown to southern Canada: the woodcock nests so very early—there are records for December in Louisiana, January in Texas, and February in North Carolina—that sometimes bird and nest together are covered up by snow, and its young may be close to flight by the time other wind birds arrive in the Arctic. A few woodcock, in favorable years, have remained as far north as Long Island, and where warm springs or other special conditions permit, the common snipe will winter north beyond the line of frozen ground; it has been found in Nova Scotia bogs in dead of winter, with the glass near zero. In mid-February of 1965, after a hard January, a lone snipe could be seen each day in a winding cattail "dreen" on the east side of Sagaponack

Pond, probing the mud (which proved to be full of tiny worms) along the very edges of the ice cakes.

Shorebirds, being highly mobile, will fly before storm or unseasonable turn of weather, but sometimes they are caught off guard by sudden freezes. On February 13 of 1899, northbound woodcock, driven back toward the south, appeared near Charleston in the tens of thousands. They were half-starved and bewildered and were killed or died. Yet species of less specialized food habits can endure very low temperatures; at Sagaponack, the sanderlings and greater yellowlegs, which are present until mid-January, will sometimes overwinter, and are usually quite common in March—though Sagaponack in the spring is a lean feeding ground for shorebirds, and even the semipalmated sandpipers, so abundant in summer and fall, mostly forsake the cold Atlantic beaches for an inland journey up the Mississippi Valley.

On the last day of April, a few years ago, there came from the sea a mixed flock of red and northern phalarope, some sixty birds in all. They rode out the two days of an easterly gale on a small pond connected to Sagaponack Pond by the small stream where I saw the winter snipe. Two red phalarope were in full nuptial plumage, bright chestnut and gold, and they led the small band which bobbed on the gray wavelets or ruffled its feathers in the salt grass, awaiting a shifting of the skies that would draw the wind birds onward to the Arctic.

FROM *The Wind Birds*

Challenging
Sea and Sky

FRED BODSWORTH

*This passage is a haunting and lyrical account of the fall mi-
gration of the Eskimo curlew, now, apparently, extinct. The last
known sighting of this bird dates from 1962. Originally, its great
migratory journey took it from its nesting grounds in the Arctic
Circle to the tip of South America and back, a distance of about
nine thousand miles. The Eskimo curlew began to decline in
the late nineteenth and early twentieth centuries with the massive destruction of the shorebirds. The great losses of migratory
bird species now taking place because of the appalling destruction of rainforests in the southern continent puts natural systems
everywhere at risk.*

*The beauty and genius of a work of art may be reconceived,
though its first material expression be destroyed; a vanished harmony may yet again inspire the composer; but when the last*

individual of a race of living beings breathes no more, another
heaven and another earth must pass before such a one can be
again. —*William Beebe*

Nights of endless flying and days of feeding at the edges of stagnant muskeg ponds followed monotonously. The green flashes of the Arctic sky's aurora borealis grew fainter behind them and they reached each dawn with hardening breast muscles that felt no fatigue. On the James Bay salt marshes food was abundant and they lingered for many days, gorging on the minute water and mud life until the southland call pressed them on again. The curlew led them straight eastward now over the ancient eroded mountains of Quebec toward the gnarled gneiss seacliffs of Labrador's Gulf of St. Lawrence.

On the second morning the dawn came in foggy and cold. There was a sharp salty tang in the heavy air that struck their nostrils and the curlew led the flock on without stopping as the dawn brightened imperceptibly into a grey, sunless day. The air warmed and the fog banks thinned and here and there brown-green patches of the bare, craggy coastal plateau began appearing between the dispersing windrows of mist below them. Then the salt tang sharpened and the fog grew thick again and the curlew knew they were nearing the seacoast. There was nothing ahead, above or below but the pressing whiteness of fog, but the curlew held course unerringly. Suddenly, towards mid-morning, the enveloping whiteness was pierced by the rumble of surf and screeching of gulls. The curlew banked sharply and dropped in a steep dive, zigzagging erratically to control the speed of descent. The plovers broke their flock formation and followed the curlew down. They leveled off a foot above water, oriented themselves with the direction of wave movement and followed the wave crests in until the cliffs broke out of the fog in a giant rock wall that towered above them. The curlew had been flying blind for several hours, but he had overshot the coast by less than a mile.

They climbed again, skimmed across the cliff top and landed. Creeping, heath-like vines of the crowberry lay everywhere and in patches the fleshy, purple berries were so thick they hid the foliage. The birds commenced feeding immediately. The wind off the sea was cold and laden with fine rain. After an hour they stopped feeding and bunched together, each bird standing with its head into the gale so that the wind carried the rain back along its overlapping feathers and off its tail.

For two weeks now there would be nothing to do but gorge and fatten for the long, non-stop flight down the Atlantic to South America. It was mid-August and the Labrador summer was already almost gone. The nights were frosty; the days were days of interminable fog. They ate crowberries until their legs and bills and plumage and excrement were stained purple with the juice. On the odd day when the fog lifted under a warming sun they flew to the beaches at low tide periods to gorge on snails and shrimps.

Every day they encountered at least one other flock of golden plovers and the curlew would stop its feeding to scan the passing flocks for another curlew like himself. There were no other curlew, no other shorebirds of any species except the plovers. But other birds were numerous. Gulls, screeching raucously into the fog, were everywhere. Long black and white lines of eider ducks were passing endlessly offshore. The stubby-winged and clumsy-flying auks and murres were still gabbling and fighting on the cliff ledges where they had raised their summer broods.

Relatively inactive now, the curlew and plovers fattened quickly. Their breasts were soft and round again with the fat layers that covered the rigid muscles beneath. August had almost ended when the old restlessness seized them again. On days when the weather cleared and the wind was right thousands of other plovers climbed high and left the coastline on a course straight south across the Gulf of St. Lawrence toward the vast Atlantic beyond. But the curlew waited, held by a tenuous bond that his meagre brain felt but couldn't quite identify. Vaguely he sensed that when the Eskimo curlews of the tundra came, they would have to come this way.

The restless urge to push on grew stronger and the curlew was torn between the two torturing desires—to wait and to move on. He found partial release from his restlessness by leading the flock on long flights up and down the coastline. Then the plovers began breaking away, joining in twos and threes with other southward flying plover flocks. The flock had dwindled to half its original size when September came and the nights grew suddenly colder. Now the fog banks which rolled in off the sea occasionally carried big, wet flakes of snow. The last plover flocks had gone. The curlew's flock was alone with the gulls and eiders.

Frost had hardened the crowberries and with their succulent juices gone the feeding had become sparser. The fat that the birds had stored up as body fuel for their ocean flight was beginning to be re-absorbed before the flight had even begun.

Finally the curlew could restrain his migratory urge no longer. On a cold dusk after a blustery day during which the temperature had barely risen above the freezing point the curlew took wing and climbed into the murky sky. The cloud ceiling was low and the flock leveled off quickly and turned seawards into a strong head wind. At this altitude it was a full gale that cut their flight speed in half. Gusts periodically broke up the flock formation. Several weaker plovers dropped behind. The curlew knew before the jagged Labrador coastline was lost to sight behind that they couldn't go on. He turned back and in a few minutes the flock alighted again on a hillside lee where the gale whined distantly overhead.

Having once started and failed, the curlew and plovers were eager now to begin the long flight. But there were no more false starts. The curlew waited restlessly for suitable weather, but the season was now late and suitable days were few. The fog dispersed but the south gale blew without break for three days and three nights while the birds fed intermittently on the drying crowberries and beach snails. On the fourth day the gale swung around the compass and continued, lighter now but colder, out of the north. This, a tail wind, was as unfavorable as the head wind had been, for it made balance in flight difficult and interfered with the delicate reflex control of the broad outer wing feathers. The north wind continued another three days, gradually weakening, until dusk of the third day when it shifted westerly and dropped to a faint breeze. This, a light cross wind, was what the curlew awaited. Night came cold and clear.

The take-off, the climb for height, the automatic V-ing with the curlew at the point were accomplished with the same casual unthinking precision as on numerous dusks before. The curlew and many of the plovers had made the ocean flight in previous autumns and they had a shadowy, remote memory of it. Most of them sensed obscurely that when dawn came there would be only the vacant sea below their wings, that they would fly on and on and another night and another dawn would come and the same vacant sea would still be there. And they knew that the sea was an alien and hostile element, for they were strictly creatures of the land and of the air. During periods of unusually smooth water they might alight briefly on the ocean's surface to snatch a few moments of rest, but they were clumsy swimmers at best, their feathers lacked oil and water-logged quickly, and rarely did the sea provide the calm conditions that would permit even a momentary landing. Usually the long flight, once begun, had to be completed non-stop without food for their stomachs or respite for their wings.

Behind them now the Arctic's aurora borealis was flashing vividly above the Labrador skyline, but when they came to earth again, with flight feathers frayed and their breast muscles numbed by fatigue, it would be in a dank jungle river-bottom of the Guianas or Venezuela. Yet there was no fear or hesitation now with the take-off, no recognition of the drama of the moment. There was only a vague relief to be off. For it was a blessing of their rudimentary brains that they couldn't see themselves in the stark perspective of reality—minute specks of earthbound flesh challenging an eternity of sea and sky.

FROM *The Last of the Curlews*

Migration:
The Corridors of Breath

BARRY LOPEZ

From the High Arctic, Barry Lopez writes of a prodigious number of birds, and the intensity and meaning with which they fill the world. The quotations with which he introduces his book are important enough to repeat in this context.

> *The landscape conveys an impression of absolute permanence. It is not hostile. It is simply there—untouched, silent and complete. It is very lonely, yet the absence of all human traces gives you the feeling you understand this land and can take your place in it.* Edmund Carpenter

> *Once in his life a man ought to concentrate his mind upon the remembered earth. He ought to give himself up to a particular landscape in his experience; to look at it from as many angles as he can, to wonder upon it, to dwell upon it.*

> *He ought to imagine that he touches it with his hands at every season and listens to the sounds that are made upon it.*

> *He ought to imagine the creatures there and all the faintest*
> *motions of the wind. He ought to recollect the glare of the*
> *moon and the colors of the dawn and dusk.*
>
> N. Scott Momaday

It was still dark, and I thought it might be raining lightly.
I pushed back the tent flap. A storm-driven sky moving
swiftly across the face of a gibbous moon. Perhaps it would
clear by dawn. The ticking sound was not rain, only the
wind. A storm, bound for somewhere else.

Half awake, I was again aware of the voices. A high-
pitched cacophonous barking, like terriers, or the complaint
of shoats. The single outcries became a rising cheer, as if in
a far-off stadium, that rose and fell away.

Snow geese, their night voices. I saw them flying down
the north coast of Alaska once in September, at the end of
a working day. The steady intent of their westward passage,
that unwavering line, was uplifting. The following year I
saw them over Banks Island, migrating north in small
flocks of twenty and thirty. And that fall I went to northern
California to spend a few days with them on their early wintering ground at Tule Lake in Klamath Basin.

Tule Lake is not widely known in America, but the
ducks and geese gather in huge aggregations on this refuge
every fall, creating an impression of land in a state of
health, of boundless life. On any given day a visitor might
look upon a million birds here—pintail, lesser scaup, Bar-
row's goldeneye, cinnamon teal, mallard, northern shoveler,
redhead, and canvasback ducks; Great Basin and cackling
varieties of Canada geese, white-fronted geese, Ross's geese,
lesser snow geese; and tundra swans. In open fields between
the lakes and marshes where these waterfowl feed and rest

are red-winged blackbirds and Savannah sparrows, Brewer's sparrows, tree swallows, and meadowlarks. And lone avian hunters—marsh hawks, red-tailed hawks, bald eagles, the diminutive kestrel.

The Klamath Basin, containing four other national wildlife refuges in addition to Tule Lake, is one of the richest habitats for migratory waterfowl in North America. To the west of Tule Lake is another large, shallow lake called Lower Klamath Lake. To the east, out past the tule marshes, is a low escarpment where barn owls nest and the counting marks of a long-gone aboriginal people are still visible, incised in the rock. To the southwest, the incongruous remains of a Japanese internment camp from World War II. In agricultural fields to the north, east, and south, farmers grow malt barley and winter potatoes in dark volcanic soils.

The night I thought I heard rain and fell asleep again to the cries of snow geese, I also heard the sound of their night flying, a great hammering of the air overhead, a wild creaking of wings. These primitive sounds made the Klamath Basin seem oddly untenanted, the ancestral ground of animals, reclaimed by them each year. In a few days at the periphery of the flocks of geese, however, I did not feel like an interloper. I felt a calmness birds can bring to people; and, quieted, I sensed here the outlines of the oldest mysteries: the nature and extent of space, the fall of light from the heavens, the pooling of time in the present, as if it were water.

There were 250,000 lesser snow geese at Tule Lake. At dawn I would find them floating on the water, close together in a raft three-quarters of a mile long and perhaps 500 yards wide. When a flock begins to rise from the surface of the water, the sound is like a storm squall arriving, a great racket of shaken sheets of corrugated tin. (If you try to separate the individual sounds in your head, they are like dry cotton towels snapping on a wind-blown clothesline.) Once airborne, they are dazzling on the wing. Flying against broken sunlight, the opaque whiteness of their bodies, a whiteness of water-polished shells, contrasts with grayer whites in their translucent wings and tail feathers. Up close they show the dense, impeccable whites of arctic fox. Against the bluish grays of a storm-laden sky, their whiteness has a surreal glow, a brilliance without shadow.

When they are feeding in the grain fields around Tule Lake, the geese come and go in flocks of five or ten thousand. Sometimes there are forty or fifty thousand in the air at once. They rise from the fields like smoke in great, swirling currents, rising higher and spreading wider in the sky than one's field of vision can encompass. One fluid, recurved sweep of ten thousand of them passes through the spaces within another, counterflying flock; while beyond them lattice after lattice passes, like sliding Japanese walls, until in the whole sky you lose your depth of field and feel as though you are looking up from the floor of the ocean through shoals of fish.

What absorbs me in these birds, beyond their beautiful whiteness, their astounding numbers, the great vigor of their lives, is how adroitly each bird joins the larger flock or departs from it. And how each bird while it is a part of the flock seems part of something larger than itself. Another animal. Never did I see a single goose move to accommodate one that was landing, nor geese on the water ever disturbed by another taking off, no matter how closely bunched they seemed to be. I never saw two birds so much as brush wingtips in the air, though surely they must. They roll up into a headwind together in a seamless movement that brings thousands of them gently to the ground like fall-

ing leaves in but a few seconds. Their movements are endlessly attractive to the eye because of a tension they create
between the extended parabolic lines of their flight and
their abrupt but adroit movements, all of it in three dimensions.

And there is something else that draws you in. They
come from the ends of the earth and find this small lake
every year with unfailing accuracy. They arrive from breeding grounds on the northern edge of the continent in Canada, and from the river valleys of Wrangel Island in the
Russian Arctic. Their ancient corridors of migration, across
Bering Strait and down the Pacific coast, down the east
flank of the Rockies, are older than the nations they fly
from. The lives of many animals are constrained by the
schemes of men, but the determination in these lives, their
traditional pattern of movement, are a calming reminder of
a more fundamental order. The company of these birds in
the field is guileless. It is easy to feel transcendent when
camped among them.

Birds tug at the mind and heart with a strange intensity.
Their ability to flock elegantly as the snow goose does,
where individual birds turn into something larger, and their
ability to navigate over great stretches of what is for us fea-
tureless space, are mysterious, sophisticated skills. Their
flight, even a burst of sparrows across a city plaza, pleases
us. In the Arctic, one can see birds in enormous numbers,
and these feelings of awe and elation are enhanced. In
spring in the Gulf of Anadyr, off the Russian coast, the surface of the water flashes silver with schools of Pacific herring, and flocks of puffins fly straight into the water after
them, like a hail of gravel. They return with the herring to
steep cliffs, where the broken shells of their offspring fall on
gusts of wind into the sea by the thousands, like snow. On

August 6, 1973, the ornithologist David Nettleship rounded Skruis Point on the north coast of Devon Island and came face to face with a "lost" breeding colony of black guillemots. It stretched southeast before him for 14 miles. On the Great Plain of the Koukdjuak on Baffin Island today, a traveler, crossing the rivers and wading through the ponds and braided streams that exhaust and finally defeat the predatory fox, will come on great windrows of feathers from molting geese, feathers that can be taken in handfuls and thrown up in the air to drift downward like chaff. From the cliffs of Digges Island and adjacent Cape Wolstenholme in Hudson Strait, 2 million thick-billed murres will swim away across the water, headed for their winter grounds on the Grand Banks.

Such enormous concentrations of life in the Arctic are, as I have suggested, temporary and misleading. Between these arctic oases stretch hundreds of miles of coastal cliffs, marshes, and riverine valleys where no waterfowl, no seabird, nests. And the flocks of migratory geese and ducks come and go quickly, laying their eggs, molting, and getting their young into the air in five or six weeks. What one witnesses in the great breeding colonies is a kind of paradox. For a time the snow and ice disappear, allowing life to flourish and birds both to find food and retrieve it. Protected from terrestrial predators on their island refuges and on nesting grounds deep within flooded coastal plains, birds can molt all their flight feathers at once, without fearing the fact that this form of escape will be lost to them for a few weeks. And, for a while, food is plentiful enough to more than serve their daily needs; it provides the additional energy needed for the molt, and for a buildup of fat reserves for the southward journey.

For the birds, these fleeting weeks of advantage are crucial. If the weather is fair and their timing has been good, they arrive on their winter grounds with a strange, primal air of achievement. When the snow geese land at Tule Lake in October, it is not necessary in order to appreciate them to picture precisely the line and shading of those few far-away places where every one of them was born—Egg River on Banks Island, the mouth of the Anderson River in the Northwest Territories, the Tundovaya River Valley on Wrangel Island. Merely knowing that each one began its life, took first breath, on those intemperate arctic edges and that it alights here now for the first or fifth or tenth time is enough. Their success urges one to wonder at such a life, stretched out over so many thousands of miles, and moving on every four or five weeks, always moving on. Food and light running out behind in the fall, looming ahead in the spring.

I would watch the geese lift off the lake in the morning, spiral up white into the blue California sky and head for fields of two-row barley to feed, able only to wonder what this kind of nomadic life meant, how their lives fit in the flow of time and made clearer the extent of space between ground and sky, between here and the Far North. They flew beautifully each morning in the directions they intended, movements of desire, arabesques in the long sweep south from Tundovaya Valley and Egg River. At that hour of the day their lives seemed flush with yearning.

One is not long in the field before sensing that the scale of time and distance for most animals is different from one's own. Their overall size, their methods of locomotion, the nature of the obstacles they face, the media they move through, and the length of a full life are all different. Formerly, because of the ready analogy with human migration and a tendency to think only on a human scale, biologists treated migratory behavior as a special event in the lives of animals. They stressed the great distances involved or remarkable feats of navigation. The practice today is not to differentiate so sharply between migration and other forms of animal (and plant) movement. The maple seed spiraling down toward the forest floor, the butterfly zigzagging across a summer meadow, and the arctic tern outward bound on its 12,000-mile fall journey are all after the same thing: an environment more conducive to their continued growth and survival. Further, scientists now understand animal movements in terms of navigational senses we are still unfamiliar with, such as an ability to detect an electromagnetic field or to use sound echoes or differences in air pressure as guides.

In discussing large-scale migration like that of snow geese, biologists posit a "familiar area" for each animal and then speak of its "home range" within that area, which includes its winter and summer ranges, its breeding range, and any migratory corridors. The familiar area takes in the whole of the landscape an animal has any notion of, an understanding it gains largely through exploration of territory adjacent to its home range during adolescence. Intense adolescent exploration, as far as we know, is common to all animals. Science's speculation is that such exploring ensures the survival of a group of animals by familiarizing them with alternatives to their home ranges, which they can turn to in an emergency.

A question that arises about the utilization of a home range is: how do animals find their way to portions of the home range they have never seen? And how do they know when going there would be beneficial? The answers to these questions still elude us, but the response to them is what we call migration, and we have some idea about how

animals manage those journeys. Many animals, even primitive creatures like anemones, possess a spatial memory of
some sort and use it to find their way in the world. Part of
this memory is apparently genetically based, and part of it
is learned during travel with parents and in exploring alone.
We know animals use a considerable range of senses to navigate from one place to another, to locate themselves in
space, and actually to *learn* an environment, but which
senses in which combinations are used, and precisely what
information is stored—so far we can only speculate.

The vision most of us have of migration is of movements
on a large scale, of birds arriving on their wintering
grounds, of spawning salmon moving upstream, or of wil-
debeest, zebra, and gazelle trekking over the plains of East
Africa. The movements of these latter animals coincide
with a pattern of rainfall in the Serengeti-Mara ecosystem;
and their annual, roughly circular migration in the wake of
the rains reveals a marvelous and intricate network of benefits to all the organisms involved—grazers, grasses, and
predators. The timing of these events—the heading of
grasses in seed, the dropping of manure, the arrival of the
rains, the birth of the young—seems perfectly fortuitous, a
melding of needs and satisfactions that caused those who
first examined the events to speak of a divine plan.

The dependable arrival of swallows at the mission of San
Juan Capistrano, the appearance of gray whales off the Or-
egon coast in March, and the movement of animals like elk
from higher to lower ranges in Wyoming in the fall are
other examples of migration familiar in North America. I
first went into the Arctic with no other ideas than these,
somewhat outsize events to guide me. They opened my
mind sufficiently, however, to a prodigious and diverse
movement of life through the Arctic; they also prompted a

realization of how intricate these seemingly simple natural events are. And as I watched the movement of whales and birds and caribou, I thought I discerned the ground from which some people have derived so much of their metaphorical understanding of symmetry, cadence, and harmony in the universe.

FROM *Arctic Dreams*

The Objects of
Immortality

PATTIANN ROGERS

If I could bestow immortality,
I'd do it liberally—on the aim of the hummingbird,
The sea nettle and the dispersing skeletons of cottonweed
In the wind, on the night heron hatchling and the night
     heron
Still bound in the blue-green darkness of its egg,
On the thrice-banded crab spider and on every low shrub
And tall teasel stem of its most perfect places.

I would ask that the turquoise skimmer, hovering
Over backwater moss, stay forever, without faltering,
Without disappearing, head half-eaten on the mud, one
     wing
Under pine rubbish, one floating downstream, nudged
And spit away by foraging darters.

And for that determination to survive,
Evident as the vibration of the manta ray beneath sand,
As the tight concentration of each trout-lily petal
On its stem, as the barbed body curled in the brain
Of the burrowing echidna, for that intensity
Which is not simply the part of the bittern's gold eye
Most easily identified and remembered but the entire
Bittern itself, for that bird-shaped realization
Of effective pressure against oblivion, I would make
My own eternal assertion: Let that pressure endure.

And maybe this immortality can come to pass
Because continuous life, even granted to every firefly
And firebeetle and fireworm on earth, to the glowing clouds
Of every deep-sea squirt, to all electric eels, phosphorescent
Fishes and scaly bright-bulbed extensions of the black
Ocean bottoms, to all luminous fungi and all torch-carrying
Creatures, to the lost light and reflective rock

Of every star in the summer sky, everlasting life,
Even granted to all of these multiplied a million times,
Could scarcely perturb or bother anyone truly
   understanding
The needs of infinity.

FROM *Splitting and Binding*

Acknowledgments

"The Dance of the Whooping Crane" by Robert Porter Allen. From *On the Trail of Vanishing Birds,* copyright © 1957 by Robert Porter Allen. Reprinted by permission of the McGraw-Hill Companies.

"The Passenger Pigeon" by John James Audubon. From *Ornithological Biography,* 1826. Reprinted from edition published 1957 by Simon & Schuster, Inc.

"Skyey Thoughts" by Mary Austin. From *The Land of Journey's Ending,* 1924. Reprinted from edition published 1983 by the University of Arizona Press.

"The Peregrine" and "Flight and Vision" by J. A. Baker. From *The Peregrine,* copyright © 1967 by J. A. Baker. Reprinted by permission of Collins Publishers, London.

"Bartram and the Birds" by William Bartram. From *The Travels of William Bartram,* 1928. Reprinted from edition published by Dover Publications, Inc.

"Bird Neighbors: The Golden-Crowned Kinglet" by Arthur Cleveland Bent. From *Life Histories of North American Thrushes, Kinglets and Their Allies,* published 1949 by the Smithsonian Institute.

"Challenging Sea and Sky" by Fred Bodsworth. From *The Last of the Curlews,* copyright © 1995 by Fred Bodsworth. Reprinted with permission of Dodd, Mead & Company.

"Bird Neighbors: The Bluebird" by John Burroughs. From *Wake-Robin,* 1871. Reprinted from edition published by Houghton Mifflin Company.

"Early Navigation: By Stars and Birds" by Rachel L. Carson. From *The Sea Around Us,* copyright © 1950, 1951, 1961 by Rachel L. Carson; renewed 1979, 1989 by Roger Christie. Reprinted by permission of Oxford University Press, Inc.

"Bird Neighbors: The Eastern Screech Owl" by Frank M. Chapman. From *Handbook of Birds of Eastern North America.* Reprinted from edition published 1966, by Dover Publications, Inc.

"The Humming Bird in Colonial America" by Hector St. John de Crèvecoeur. From *Letters from an American Farmer,* 1782. Reprinted from edition published 1926 by E. P. Dutton & Company. Reprinted by permission of J. M. Dent & Sons, London.

"The Andean Condor" by Charles Darwin. From *The Voyage of the Beagle,* 1839. Reprinted from edition published 1989 by Viking Penguin.

"Spring" by Annie Dillard. From *Pilgrim at Tinker Creek,* copyright © 1974 by Annie Dillard. Reprinted by permission of HarperCollins Publishers, Inc.

"Bird Neighbors: The Black-Capped Chickadee" and "Bird Neighbors: The Loon; Or, Great Northern Diver" by Edward Howe Forbush. From *Birds of Massachusetts and Other New England States,* 1929. Published by Erwich & Smith Company.

"From Another World" by Louis J. Halle. From *The Storm Petrel and the Owl of Athena,* copyright © 1970 by Louis J. Halle. Reprinted by permission of Princeton University Press.

"The Light-Mantled Sooty Albatross" by Louis J. Halle. From *The Sea and the Ice, a Naturalist in Antarctica,* copyright © 1973 by Louis J. Halle. Reprinted by permission of Houghton Mifflin Company.

"Bird Song Compared to Human Music" by Charles Hartshorne. From *Born to Sing,* copyright © 1973 by Charles Hartshorne. Reprinted by permission of Indiana University Press.

"Ritual in Terns" by John Hay. From *The Bird of Light,* copyright © 1991 by John Hay. Reprinted by permission of W. W. Norton & Company, Inc.

"A Raven's Call" by Bernd Heinrich. From *Ravens in Winter,* copyright © 1989 by Bernd Heinrich. Published by Summit Books.

"The Windhover" by Gerard Manley Hopkins. From *A Gerard Manley Hopkins Reader,* ed. John Pick. Reprinted from edition published 1953 by Oxford University Press.

"The Kingfisher" by Ted Hughes. From *The River,* copyright © 1983 by Ted Hughes. Reprinted by permission of Faber and Faber, Ltd., London.

"Wild Swans of the Chesapeake" by Gilbert Klingel. From *The Bay,* copyright © 1951 by Gilbert Klingel. Reprinted with permission of Dodd, Mead & Company.

"The Road Runner" by Joseph Wood Krutch. From *The Voice of the Desert,* 1955. Reprinted from edition published 1980 by William Morrow & Company.

"Birds Sowing and Harvesting" by Ted Levin. From *Blood Brook,* copyright © 1992 by Ted Levin. Reprinted with permission from Chelsea Green Publishing Company, White River Junction, Vermont.

"Migration: The Corridors of Breath" by Barry Lopez. From *Arctic Dreams,* copyright © 1986 by Barry Lopez. Published by permission of Charles Scribner's Sons, a division of Simon & Schuster, Inc.

"Playing with the Wind" by Konrad Lorenz. From *King Solomon's Ring,* 1952. Reprinted from edition published by New American Library, 1952.

"Birds and the Flute: The Pipes of Pan" by Lucretius, tr. by Russel M. Geer. From *On Nature,* published by Howard W. Sams & Company, Inc., 1965.

"Migration of the Shorebirds" by Peter Matthiessen. From *The Wind Birds*, copyright © 1973 by Peter Matthiessen. Reprinted by permission of Viking Penguin, Inc.

"The Frigate Pelican" by Marianne Moore. From *The Complete Poems of Marianne Moore*, copyright © 1967 by Marianne Moore. Published by the Viking Press and reprinted by permission of Lydia Zelaya.

"The Water Ouzel" by John Muir. From *The Mountains of California*, 1911.

"Wideawake Fair" and "The Brown Skua" by Robert Cushman Murphy. From *The Oceanic Birds of South America, Vol. I*, 1936. Published by the American Museum of Natural History.

"Where the Birds Are Our Friends" by Gary Paul Nabhan. From *The Desert Smells Like Rain (A Naturalist in Papago Indian Country)*, copyright © 1982 by Gary Paul Nabhan and published by North Point Press. Reprinted by permission of Farrar, Straus & Giroux, Inc.

"The Loon" by Richard K. Nelson. From *Make Prayers to the Raven*, copyright © 1983 by Richard K. Nelson. Reprinted by permission of the University of Chicago Press.

"The Wandering Albatross" and "Migration" by Pablo Neruda. From *The Art of Birds*, by Pablo Neruda, tr. by Jack Schmitt, copyright © 1985. Reprinted by permission of the University of Texas Press.

"Visions and Flight" by Charlton Ogburn. From *The Adventures of Birds*, by Charlton Ogburn, copyright © 1976. Reprinted by permission of William Morrow & Company, Inc.

"In the Pinewoods, Crows and Owl" by Mary Oliver. From *American Primitives*, copyright © 1983 by Mary Oliver. Reprinted by permission of Little, Brown & Company.

"The Terns" by Mary Oliver. From *House of Light*, copyright © 1990 by Mary Oliver. Reprinted by permission of Beacon Press, Boston.

"Our Lads" and "Duck Weather" by Jake Page. From *Songs to Birds*, copyright © 1993 by Jake Page. Reprinted by permission of David R. Godine Publisher, Inc.

by Niko Tinbergen. Reprinted by permission of Harper-Collins Publishers, Inc.

"Sea-Going of the Murre Chicks" by Leslie M. Tuck. From *The Murres*, copyright © 1960 by Leslie M. Tuck.

"The Aesthetic Sense" by Karl Von Frisch. From *Animal Architecture*, copyright © 1974 by Karl Von Frisch and Otto Von Frisch. Reprinted by permission of Harcourt Brace & Company.

"To the Man-of-War Bird" by Walt Whitman. From *The Complete Poetry & Selected Prose and Letters by Walt Whitman*, ed. Emory Holloway. Reprinted by permission of Random House, Inc.

"Kokopelli: Symbol of a Continent of Birds" by Terry Tempest Williams. From *Coyote Canyon*, copyright © 1989 by Terry Tempest Williams. Reprinted by permission of Peregrine Smith Books.

"Emperor Penguins" by Edward A. Wilson. From *Diary of the Discovery Expedition to the Antarctic 1901–1904*. Reprinted from edition published 1967 by Humanities Press International, Inc.

"Evolution and the Bird of Paradise" by Edward O. Wilson. From *Biophilia*, copyright © 1984 by Edward O. Wilson. Reprinted by permission of Harvard University Press.